DATE DUE

JAN 1 3 2006	

PLAYBOY

Guide to Playing Poker at Home

PLAYBOY

Guide to Playing Poker at Home

Basil Nestor

Illustrations by LeRoy Neiman

Sterling Publishing Co., Inc.
New York

Published by Sterling Publishing Co., Inc.

387 Park Avenue South, New York, NY 10016

Text ©2004 by Basil Nestor
This edition 2004 by Sterling Publishing Co., Inc.

Playboy and Rabbit Head design are trademarks of Playboy Enterprises International, Inc.

Distributed in Canada by Sterling Publishing
c/o Canadian Manda Group, 165 Dufferin Street,
Toronto, Ontario, Canada M6K 3H6

Distributed in Great Britain by Chrysalis Books
64 Brewery Road, London N79NT, England

Distributed in Australia by Capricorn Link (Australia) Pty. Ltd.
P.O. Box 704, Windsor, NSW 2756, Australia

This book contains the opinions and ideas of its author, and it is designed to provide useful advice to the reader on the subject of playing poker at home. The publisher, licensor, and author specifically disclaim responsibility for any liability, loss, or risk (financial, personal, or otherwise) that may be claimed or incurred as a consequence, directly or indirectly, of the use and/or application of the contents of this book.

  The publisher, licensor, and author assume no responsibility for errors or omissions. They do not attest to the validity, accuracy, or completeness of this information. The strategies in this book are not guaranteed or warranted to produce any particular result. Use of a term in this book should not be regarded as affecting the validity of any trademark or service mark. This book is for informational purposes and in no way represents an inducement to gamble.

ISBN 1-4027-2040-8

Designed by Jeffrey Rutzky

Femlin illustrations by LeRoy Neiman
Additional illustrations by Jeffrey Rutzky

Printed in China by SNP Excel

10 9 8 7 6 5 4 3 2 1

This book is dedicated to Miracle Novel,
a most unusual and memorable person.

Acknowledgments

Thanks to my editors Nathaniel Marunas
and Betsy Beier. They understand the
spirit of poker. Thanks to Fay Nestor
for her love and patience.

Special thanks and kudos to
Sharyn Rosart. Her positive energy
has influenced me (and my readers)
in so many wonderful ways.

CONTENTS

PART THREE Seven-Card Stud and Other Games

PART FOUR Practical Issues

INTRODUCTION
Playing Poker
vs.
Winning Poker

Before we get started, let me ask you an important question:

Is it okay if you lose $500 or $1,000 the next time you sit down to play poker? Will you finish the evening in a good mood? Consider the following statement: "I'm just glad that I played the game. Poker for me is mostly about camaraderie. Winning or losing is a minor issue." Do you agree? Is losing really okay?

To anyone who answers yes to the above, I offer this advice: Read the first two chapters of this book, skim the rest if you have the time, but don't bother too much with the strategies and the nuances of the games. Just cut loose and go wild! Have a great time. Your poker pals will love you. You'll be the hit of every party, and you'll be sought after at poker gatherings throughout your geographic area.

In addition to making you very popular, this "go wild" approach will save you precious time. In the next hour or so you'll be ready to play poker in any venue on earth. No muss, no fuss. Party on!

Okay?

On the other hand, if your idea of fun does *not* include toasting five or ten Ben Franklins per session, if you'd like to save that money and maybe win some dollars off your opponents, then you'll have to read this whole book a few times.

And if you want to play poker in a casino (and you want to win), then you'll probably have to read a few more books. And you'll have to practice, too.

I mention this because the strategies presented here require effort. They're not especially complicated or difficult, but it's like servicing a car or practicing a golf swing; you've got to actually do it to see the results.

Also, poker is a game of nuances; seemingly small changes can have big consequences. If you want to win, then you have to care about these differences, and you must understand how these differences can affect the texture of the game.

The first and most important difference is that poker played at home (private poker) is fundamentally different from poker played in a casino (public poker). There are a number of reasons for this.

Poker in Casinos

Casinos are open all day, every day of the year. There's no need to organize a game or wait for Thursday night. You can win as much as you want without worrying about busting out Grandpa or bankrupting your brother-in-law. You can leave the table when you're ready to stop, or play as long as you like when everyone else wants to quit; new players will be waiting to join the game. Rules in casinos are enforced by professional dealers and supervisors. Security guards patrol the casino and the parking lot. You don't even need to bring cash or a check; there's an ATM machine just a few steps away.

Casinos have lush surroundings, chandeliers, supervisors in tuxedos... And did I mention the gourmet meals? In the better casinos, you can order a top-quality meal and have it delivered right to the table. Oh, the pleasure of dining on foie gras! Especially when you pay for it with chips from a pot you just won.

Sounds great, right? Well, as great as casinos are, they have some drawbacks. First, not everyone lives near a casino. A private game at a neighbor's house may be more appealing than schlepping one hundred miles to another county. Second, the casino charges money to pay for the dealers, cards, table, chandeliers, free soft drinks, and so forth. The charge is typically about $10 to $15 an hour, and it's collected as a fee from winners, or as a seat charge.

The third and biggest drawback to poker in casinos is that sometimes you run into players who are really good. They're way better than Grandpa or your brother-in-law. These players will slice, dice, and serve you like salmon on a bagel (or maybe foie gras). Mind you, I'm *not* saying you can't beat these guys with some practice. My point here is that you can usually avoid them altogether when you organize a private game.

Oh…and there's a fourth drawback to casinos. Sometimes when you win, opponents get angry. They curse you (or the dealer). They throw cards. They behave in ways that can be very unpleasant. Of course, the casino will eject players who become too obnoxious. So the smarter "maniacs" control their belligerence just enough to avoid ejection. They mutter, they give you dirty looks, they complain about your style of play, or accuse you of breaking the rules. Their purpose is to put you on tilt, get you flustered so you lose concentration and play poorly. This type of psychological warfare doesn't happen all the time, or even most of the time. But it does happen.

Have I made casino poker sound horrible? It's not. Go back and reread the first two paragraphs of this section.

There are *a lot* of advantages to playing poker in casinos. The point here is that it's a *different game* from playing poker at home.

Poker at Home

When you play poker at home, you supply the cards, the chips, the table, and venue. It's your game, so there are practical issues you must consider. For example, you must handle cash and debts. You and the other players must enforce the rules. Who will be allowed into the game? What will be the betting limits? How will disputes be settled? What happens if someone cheats?

It's no accident that poker games in private venues have been the grist for crime novels and movie scripts since... well...since crime novels and movie scripts were invented.

Of course, you don't have to worry about cheating or a shoot-out over a poker hand if it's just you playing with friends (unless your name is Tony Soprano or Wyatt Earp). But the larger issue here is that *you are running a game.*

If you're really into winning, you must carefully choose opponents who are bad poker players. Some poker hosts milk their opponents once a week like cows. But doing this takes some finesse. You've got to extract the money gently and let chronic losers win every so often.

And sometimes, poker gatherings *really are* genuinely about camaraderie. In those situations, you play your best, enjoy the company, and try to beat your opponents in the spirit of healthy competition.

And speaking of beating your opponents, the *biggest difference* between playing in a casino and playing at home involves the actual strategies for winning. A profitable strategy in a casino will not necessarily work at home, and the same is true when using home strategies in a casino.

The reasons for this involve many factors, such as the number of people in a hand and the degree to which they're willing to risk money. Betting limits are also a factor. I'll discuss these issues in later chapters. Right now just remember that the strategies in this book apply mostly to playing poker at home.

You can certainly extrapolate some of these strategies to casino poker, but if you want to play in a casino, I recommend you purchase *The Smarter Bet*™ *Guide to Poker* (Sterling Publishing). It's loaded with tactics to help you beat casino sharks. Eventually, you'll be serving *them* up on bagels...while you're dining on foie gras.

In this book, let's focus on grilled cheese sandwiches, ham and turkey clubs, or my favorite...tuna melts. Mmmmmm! You turn the page, I'll hit the fridge, and then we'll start learning about playing poker at home.

PART ONE

Basic Concepts

CHAPTER 1

Poker Fundamentals

A lottery ticket usually costs a dollar, right? Imagine if you could pay a penny and buy just the first two numbers on a lottery ticket. If those numbers miss, then you could throw the ticket away and save ninety-nine cents.

But what if those two numbers hit? Imagine now that the lottery drawing would be stopped long enough to give you a chance to buy additional numbers for a nickel. If those numbers miss, you can throw the ticket away. If the extra numbers hit, then the lottery drawing is stopped once again. You're allowed to pay ninety-four cents (the balance of the full price) to draw for the last number. Wouldn't that be an amazing advantage?

Unfortunately, there's no lottery contest in the world that will allow you to play this way.

But a poker contest will. That's right. You can use this strategy to play poker.

Luck vs. Skill

We'll explore the lottery analogy more in later chapters, but right now just remember that a "preview" system exists in poker, and many players don't quite realize it. Some do, but they have an incomplete understanding of how it works. Only a small percentage of players fully comprehend the system and all its ramifications.

This uneven distribution of knowledge is a critical factor in the game. Poker players have widely varying levels of competence (or incompetence). This makes poker very different from most gambling games. In fact, poker is more like...well...golf.

Yes, it sounds strange, but it's true. Think about it. Golf is a game in which people compete with each other. But how often do guys get together to compete over slots or baccarat? Do you and your pals play roulette after work? Probably not. Most gambling games put an individual on one side, and a casino (or the state) is on the other side.

Expert players can squeeze out a positive edge against a casino in some situations, but in most contests the house has an overwhelming advantage. That's why there are no gambling professionals who earn a living playing roulette, slots, keno, or craps. It's not mathematically possible to win at those games in the long run.

There are a few people who earn a living playing blackjack, and even fewer who sustain themselves playing video poker, but it's tough. Perfect play will produce about a 1 percent player edge. Skill is important in those contests, but luck still holds a tremendous sway.

It's the other way around in poker. Luck has an influence, but skill has a more pronounced effect. The opponent isn't a monolithic casino with a built-in advantage. Instead, there are multiple opponents with varying levels of expertise. Some are very good, but most are casual players with average to marginal skill. They enjoy the game and play with their friends once a week, or a few times a year. Doesn't that sound like golf?

Poker even has a tournament circuit (as you've surely noticed if you watch the World Poker Tour). Pros make the rounds to earn their living. There are big-money events and smaller contests. Beginners often compete with champions, just as they do in a golf pro-am.

Understanding the similarities between poker and golf and the fundamental differences between poker and most other gambling contests is important for many reasons. First, your money is potentially at *greater* risk when playing poker than it is when playing typical gambling games. The house edge (built-in casino advantage) slowly bleeds you dry in most gambling contests, but it protects you as well. The mathematics are set. Sometimes you win and more times they win. Not so in poker. If you're a beginner or someone who relies mostly on luck, and you unwittingly play against someone who has greater skill, it's like playing eighteen holes against Tiger Woods. You'll consistently lose.

And remember that expert poker players don't wear signs or black hats. They're your buddies, neighbors, relatives, co-workers. But they take your money. Uncle Lou from Peoria, Janice from the office, Stan from across the street...will suck the Andy Jacksons straight out of your wallet.

You don't want that to happen. And this brings us to the most important issue in poker...

The Object of the Game

Poker can be played for just about anything of value, including matches, pennies, clothing, or property. But the most typical prize is money. Poker is about money. That is the object of the game.

The object of poker *is not* to have a superior hand or to frequently beat your opponents. In fact, players with the strongest hands often win the smallest amounts. And players who consistently win more hands than their opponents are usually people who finish with a net loss.

Does that sound confusing? I'll explain how it works as we go along, but right now just remember...

The goal in poker is to win the most money.

> ***"If you can't spot the sucker in your first half-hour at the table, then you're the sucker."***
>
> —Mike McDermott (played by Matt Damon) in *Rounders*

Everything we cover, every element of the game, every decision you make, every moment at the table is entirely about this one purpose. Never let yourself be distracted by any other poker goals. Beating your opponent, exposing a bluff, winning a long shot, or stacking a big pile of chips can all be tremendous fun, but they won't necessarily make you a poker winner.

Of course, having fun is important. Life is too short to have a bad time, but if you allow transitory fun to supersede profit then you'll be a pleasure-seeking loser. Players in this mind-set are referred to as live ones, and they are beloved and welcome in any poker gathering (most especially mine). They prefer mindless risk to reward. A heart-thumping challenge is what turns them on. If they can't win a lot, then they want to lose a lot. God bless 'em!

Nick the Greek, the famous gambler, once said, "The next best thing to gambling and winning is gambling and losing." He won millions over the course of his career. And he died broke. Enough said.

Players, Pot, and Showdown

The two most popular poker versions are Texas hold 'em (often just called hold 'em) and seven-card stud. Other common versions include Omaha hi/lo and pineapple. All are played with a standard fifty-two-card deck. We'll cover these versions and a few more later. Right now we're going to focus on the common elements of every genuine poker contest.

All genuine poker games have multiple players, typically four to nine people, competing to win a single pot (the combined bets of all the players). The pile of money increases as cards are dealt and players with strong poker hands (or bluffers representing strong hands) bet into the pot. Other players must match the bets or give up, thus losing whatever money they have invested.

The contest ends when everyone concedes to one player, or when two or more players match bets in the final round and there is a showdown. The remaining players reveal their hands and compare them. The person with the best poker hand wins the pot.

Note that poker-based contests such as video poker, pai gow poker, Let It Ride, Three Card Poker, Caribbean Stud Poker, and many other recently developed games don't have all three of these basic poker elements (multiple players, a pot, and a showdown). Quasi-poker games are certainly fun to play, but they're closer in function to craps and blackjack than traditional poker, so we don't cover them in this book.

Ranking the Hands

Poker hands are ranked in winning order as follows:

Royal Flush: Ace, king, queen, jack, and ten of the same suit. A royal flush can be made four different ways, but you'll be lucky if you see one in a lifetime.

Straight Flush: Five cards of the same suit in exactly adjacent ranks. Another example would be **5♦ 4♦ 3♦ 2♦ A♦**. Note that an ace is used to make the lowest straight flush.

Four of a Kind: Four cards of the same rank and a fifth card of any rank and suit.

Full House: Three cards of the same rank and a pair of another rank.

Flush: Five cards of the same suit that are not exactly adjacent ranks.

Straight: Five cards not of the same suit in exactly adjacent ranks. An ace is used to make both the highest and the lowest straight.

Three of a Kind: Three cards of the same rank and two cards of different ranks.

Two Pairs: Two cards of one rank, two cards of another rank, and a fifth card of a third rank.

One Pair: Two cards of one rank and three cards of different ranks.

No Pair: Five cards that don't make any combination.

Exactly five cards are used to determine a winner, no less and no more. Even though a five-card hand may be built from seven or more cards (depending on the game), those extra cards don't count in a showdown.

When two or more hands of the same rank (two straights, two flushes, etc.) are in a showdown, the high cards in each hand determine the winner. For example, a queen-high straight flush beats a ten-high straight flush. Three kings beat three jacks. A pair of aces beats a pair of queens. An ace-high flush beats a flush that has a high card of nine. If both players have identical combinations (both have two kings and two aces), then the highest fifth card in the hand determines the winner. This lone card is known as a **kicker**

Full houses are judged first by the three matching cards and then by the pair, so kings full of jacks (three kings and two jacks) beats queens full of aces.

If neither hand makes a pair, then the hand with the highest card wins. If that card is matched, then the next card is used to decide, and so on. The pot is split when all five cards match in rank. Suit is never used to determine a winner. The order of the cards has no importance.

What are the chances that your trips (three of a kind) will be beaten by a straight? The following table shows the total number of possible five-card card combinations that can be dealt from a fifty-two-card deck.

THE FACT IS...

Some versions of poker (like **razz**) are played for low, meaning that the worst hand wins. It sounds easy, but it's tougher than you might think. You have an equal probability of being dealt the best hand or the worst hand. For more on razz, see Chapter 9.

Frequency of Poker Hands

Hand	Number of Occurrences	Percent Probability
Royal Flush	4	0.00015%
Straight Flush	36	0.0014
Four-of-a-kind	624	0.02
Full House	3,744	0.14
Flush	5,108	0.20
Straight	10,200	0.39
Three-of-a-kind	54,912	2.11
Two Pair	123,552	4.75
One Pair	1,098,240	42.26
Everything Else	1,302,540	50.12
Total	2,598,960	

The column on the far right shows the probability of receiving any particular hand when exactly five cards are dealt. It's somewhat easier to make a hand with seven cards (as in hold 'em or seven-card stud), but two pairs or better still constitute less than **39** percent of seven-card hands.

Remember, the actual probability of getting any hand changes as the cards are revealed. For example, if you already have four cards to a flush, then the chance of finishing with a flush is significantly higher. And it's easier to make a hand when using more than five cards (as in hold 'em and seven-card stud). Nevertheless, you may go a lifetime without seeing a "natural" royal flush.

Now you know what beats what. In the next chapter I'll show you how Texas hold 'em is played.

Essentially

♠ Poker is different from most gambling games because the opponent in poker is not a casino; the opponents are other players who have various skill levels.

♥ The object in poker is to win the most money. Winning the most pots or having the best hand is not necessarily the best way to win the most money.

♦ All genuine poker games have multiple players competing to win a single pot. Opponents either concede to one player, or there is a showdown where two or more players reveal their hand. The person with the best poker hand wins the pot.

♣ Poker-hand rankings reflect the probability that a particular hand will appear in a randomly dealt five-card combination. Higher hands occur less frequently.

CHAPTER 2

An Introduction to Hold 'Em

If you watch the World Poker Tour, then you're probably somewhat familiar with hold 'em. It's been around since the mid-twentieth century, and it has become wildly popular in recent years.

If you don't watch the World Poker Tour, don't worry. I'll thoroughly explain hold 'em in the next few pages. But first, I want to briefly mention two other classic poker versions, five-card draw and seven-card stud. We'll cover them in Part Three of this book. I'm mentioning them here because, once upon a time, each was the dominant poker version. Five-card draw was popular in the Old West (that's why you see it so often in old movies). Seven-card stud was the dominant version through most of the twentieth century.

You might be familiar with these games and you might wonder why we're starting instead with hold 'em.

Mostly, it's because hold 'em (and its cousins Omaha hi/lo and pineapple) represent the latest trend in poker. They're known as **flop games**.

Part of the reason for the growing dominance of flop games is that they're faster and somewhat easier to play than seven-card stud and five-card draw, yet they're no less responsive to strategy. Also, Texas hold 'em is the game that determines the world champion in the annual World Series of Poker.

All of these factors make hold 'em an ideal "learning" version. So this book begins with hold 'em, and then we move on to seven-card stud, five-card draw, and other versions.

Also remember, many of the strategies in the hold 'em chapters apply to *all* genuine poker contests. You'll be four-fifths of the way to knowing every poker version on earth by the time we get to Part Three of this book.

Community Cards

Each player receives only two cards in hold 'em. They are dealt face down. During the course of play, five additional cards are dealt face up on the board (the table) as community cards; these are shared by all the players. We'll cover betting and raising in a later section; for right now just remember that players use the community cards and their two pocket cards (hole cards) to build a five-card poker hand. A final hand can include one, both, or in some circumstances none of the pocket cards.

It's probably very different from the poker games you've seen in the movies (unless you've seen *Rounders*), but this is how modern poker is played.

Let's say you have:

Your opponent has:

And the board shows:

You have a king-high flush (K♠ J♠ T♠ 9♠ 2♠), and your opponent has a king-high straight (K♥ Q♦ J♣ T♠ 9♠), You would win this hand in a showdown. If you hold:

Your opponent has:

And the board shows:

You have a full house, kings full of aces, but your opponent has a higher full house, aces full of kings.

Here is a bad beat example from a hand I once played. I was holding:

My opponent was holding:

The board showed:

My ace-high flush was beaten by a jack-high straight flush, and my opponent used only one card from his hand to do it.

The concept of community cards may seem odd at first, but you'll soon realize that it's an advantage for observant players because reading your

> **"I'd equate it with chess or other games of skill that require multilevel strategic, mathematical, or psychological skills. For the people who play it seriously, there's no luck involved at all."**
>
> —Edward Norton, on his role in *Rounders*

opponent's hand is much easier in an open game (some cards dealt face up) than in a closed game (no cards revealed) like five-card draw.

For example, a full house is not possible in hold 'em unless there is a pair on the board. A flush is not possible unless the board has three suited cards. A straight is not possible unless three cards on the board are within five ranks of one another.

Holding the Nuts

The straight flush in the previous section is an unbeatable hand. In other words, a higher hand is not possible with that particular combination of cards on the board. The person who holds an unbeatable combination is said to be holding the nuts.

Recognizing when you have the nuts (or when you don't) is an important part of profitable poker. Going back through the examples, the nuts for A♦ K♥ 3♠ A♠ 9♦ are AA unless you're holding one ace, in which case the nuts are AK (making a full house). No higher hand is possible.

For J♣ T♠ 2♠ 8♦ 9♠, the nuts are an ace of spades and any other spade. The ace creates a nut flush, a flush that cannot be beaten (because a straight flush is not possible with this particular board).

A straight made with an ace would be a nut straight. For example, when the board shows K♣ Q♥ 6♦ J♦ 5♣, the nuts are any hand with an ace and ten.

Betting, Raising, and Folding

You're probably familiar with the concept of an ante. It's a small bet made by all the players in a hand to start the pot. This puts money in play, and it makes additional bets worth the risk.

Five-card draw and seven-card stud use antes, but hold 'em doesn't. Instead it uses a rotating system of blind bets to start the pot. Each player is designated in turn as dealer for one hand (the dealer position moves clockwise around the table). The two players to the left of the dealer must make blind bets to start the pot. The first player to the left of the dealer makes a small blind bet, which is less than the table minimum. The exact amount varies depending on the game, but it's usually half of the minimum bet. The second player makes a big blind bet, which is usually the table minimum. Some games have just one blind.

The dealer confirms that the blinds have been posted (placed on the table), then she shuffles the cards and begins the hand. We'll get into the specifics of shuffling and dealing in the next chapter.

Cards are dealt clockwise starting to the left of the dealer. Each player receives two cards dealt face down (one card to everyone in the hand, and then a second card to everyone in the hand). Players carefully lift the cards, look at them, then put them back on the table. There are rules for handling cards that we'll cover in the next chapter, but the important thing to remember here is that you'll generally look at the cards once, and they'll remain face down through the rest of the hand.

The first action (opportunity to act) begins with the person to the left of the big blind. That player has three options:

Fold: This is an unconditional surrender. The player returns his cards to the dealer and is out of the hand. No bet is required.

Call: Match the previous bet (in this case it's the bet posted by the big blind). This allows the player to stay in the game and continue playing for the pot.

Raise: Bet more than the previous bet (see the next section for info re betting limits). A raise allows the player to remain in the game, and it requires everyone else to call the increased amount, raise, or fold.

 **Tip**

Action in the first round of hold 'em always begins with the first player to the left of the big blind, and it proceeds clockwise until all the players have called or folded to a single player. In later rounds, action always begins with the first active player to the left of the dealer.

A fourth option is sometimes used in later rounds. It is...

Check: Neither bet nor fold. The action passes to the next player. This option is available only when a bet has not yet been made. Players who check and subsequently raise a later bet in the same round have performed a check-raise. It's an aggressive move that is prohibited in some private games.

Betting Limits

Games are defined by the type of poker (seven-card stud, hold 'em, etc.) and by betting limits, 3-6, 6-12, 10-20, or some other combination of numbers. In a fixed-limit game the first number is the dollar amount that can be bet or raised in the early rounds (usually rounds one and two); the second number is the amount that can be bet or raised in later rounds. A spread-limit game allows any bet between two amounts at any time. No-limit means just what it says; any amount can be bet at any time (very dangerous for beginners). Pot-limit means that any amount up to the current value of the pot can be bet at any time. The strategy examples in this book apply to fixed-limit games unless otherwise stated.

Most games have a required minimum buy-in. This is a minimum amount that you must put at risk to sit in the game. It's usually at least five times the maximum bet of that particular game ($40 for a 4-8 game). You're better off buying in for at least three to five times that amount. I'll explain why in a later section.

Anatomy of a Poker Hand

Now let's put it all together. Here's an example of how a hand in a 3-6 game might develop. There are seven players at the table. The big blind is $3 and the little blind is $2.

Before the Flop

Mickey is under the gun; he is sitting to the left of the big blind, and he's the first player to act. Mickey calls the big blind with a bet of $3. Sandy is on Mickey's left; he raises $3 for a total wager of $6. Luke (to the left of Sandy) must either call the $6 wager, fold, or raise another $3 to make it $9. Luke raises. Each of the other players must either put in $9, fold, or raise again.

Two players (including the dealer) fold after Luke and the action moves to Chris, the little blind. He's already got $2 in the pot. So he must put in an additional $7, fold, or raise. He folds.

Erin is the big blind. She raises another $3 for a total bet of $12. This particular game has a cap of three raises per round, so everyone remaining in the hand must either call $12 or fold. No more raises are allowed.

The action moves back to Mickey, the original caller.

Tip

You should stick to low-limit games until you're a consistent winner. Start with 2-4, 3-6, or 4-8. Don't go above 6-12 until you're entirely satisfied with your performance at the lower limits.

He decides that his hand was worth $3 but not $12, and he folds. Sandy and Luke call. The pot is now $41.

There are three players left in the hand: Erin, Sandy, and Luke.

The Flop

After everyone has either called or folded, the dealer burns the top card from the deck (removes that card from play without revealing it). This is a standard security measure to prevent cheating. We'll talk more about it in Chapter 3.

The next three cards in the deck are dealt face up on the table. This is known as the flop. The board shows:

The first active player to the left of the dealer starts the betting in this round and in every subsequent round.

That would be Erin in this example. She checks. Sandy bets $3. Luke folds. Erin raises to $6 (a check-raise). Ouch! Sandy now wonders if Erin is suckering him or bluffing. Sandy is holding:

That gives him two pairs (aces and kings). There are only three hands that Erin could be holding to beat Sandy at this point; **AA**, **KK**, or **44** would give her three of a kind. Sandy calls, "Time." This is a verbal declaration requesting a pause in the action.

Sandy thinks it over. Perhaps Erin is holding a combination that he can currently beat or tie (**AK**, **AQ**, **AJ**, etc.). He

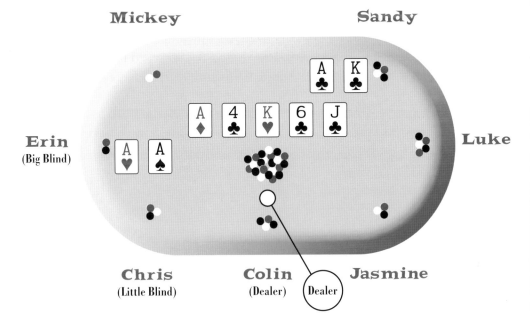

Mickey

Sandy

Erin
(Big Blind)

Luke

Chris
(Little Blind)

Colin
(Dealer)

Dealer

Jasmine

Sandy wins with a flush over Erin's three aces. Colin was the dealer for this hand. Chris was the little blind. Erin was the big blind. Mickey was under the gun (first to act before the flop). Erin was the first live player to the left of the dealer after the flop, so she started action on the flop, turn, and river. Chris will be the dealer for the next hand.

decides to test her hand with a reraise. Sandy puts another $6 in the pot (matching Erin's raise and adding an extra $3).

Erin raises again. Sandy decides she has a set (trips made with a pocket pair), or if she doesn't have a set…then she's just a maniac. He calls. The total in the pot is now $65.

The Turn and the River

The dealer burns another card, and a fourth card is revealed. This round is known as the turn. Betting levels are double the previous rounds.

The turn card is 6♣. Sandy still has

THE FACT IS…

If players call the big blind but none of them raise, then the big blind can check and end the first round of betting, or "raise herself" when the action comes around.

two pairs, but now he's got four cards to a club flush. Erin bets $6. Sandy calls. The pot swells to $77.

Another burned card, and the last card is revealed. It's a J♣. This round is called the **river**. The board shows:

Remember that Sandy is holding A♣ K♣, so his hand has improved to an ace-high club flush. There is no pair on the board, and that means a full house is not possible. Sandy has the nuts. Erin checks. Sandy bets $6. Erin calls. The betting is concluded. The dealer asks both players to reveal their hands for the showdown. Sandy flips up his ace and king. Erin turns over A♥ A♠. She was winning with trips until the last card. Sandy rakes in $89. The cards pass clockwise to the next dealer, and a new hand begins.

Sandy's profit was $53 ($89 less his contribution of $36). Erin lost $36. Luke lost $12. Mickey lost $3. Chris lost $2. The other players folded before contributing anything to the pot.

Analysis of the Action

A showdown like that gets your heart thumping. Stacking the chips makes you feel ten feet tall, and being the loser makes you wonder if the poker gods hate you. But Sandy and Erin are both good players. They'll think about the hand before taking credit or assigning blame.

Here's the beautiful part. Both of them will conclude that they played their hands properly (which they both did), and that Luke and Chris also probably made correct choices, but the person who made the mistake was Mickey. He either called with a weak hand, or improperly threw away a strong one. Of course, he lost only $3, but it's the little leaks that eventually sink the battleship bankroll. Also, Mickey revealed valuable information about his lack of expertise. Sandy and Erin will use that profitably for the rest of the evening.

Now you might be saying, "Wait a second. Luke raised and then folded. He lost four times as much as Mickey. Didn't he make a mistake?"

Nope. He played his hand perfectly.

I'll explain why in Chapter 4, but first let's finish our review of the general rules of the game, and we'll discuss issues such as shuffling, dealing, and burning cards.

> *"You're good, kid, but as long as I'm around you're second best. You might as well learn to live with it."*
>
> —Lancey Howard (played by Edward G. Robinson), in *The Cincinnati Kid*

Essentially

♠ Poker games are identified by the game type, the dollar-amount betting limits, and the betting structure (fixed-limit, spread-limit, pot-limit, or no limit).

♥ Hold 'em and seven-card stud are the most popular poker versions. Other well-known versions such as Omaha hi/lo and pineapple are based on hold 'em.

♦ Hold 'em players use two personal cards and five shared community cards to build a five-card poker hand. The game has four rounds: pre-flop, flop, turn, and river.

♣ If a bet has not yet been made, players have two options when action reaches them; they can check or bet. If a bet has been made, then a player can fold, call, or raise.

♠ A player who holds an unbeatable hand is said to be holding "the nuts." Recognizing when you have the nuts (or when you don't) is an important part of profitable poker.

CHAPTER 3

Rules and Customs for Poker at Home

Poker is like any organized activity; it works best when everyone follows the rules. Sloppy play causes confusion and delays. It can change the outcome of a hand, and it generally makes everyone uncomfortable and unhappy. That's why every poker player has a responsibility to uphold and maintain the integrity of the game.

But it's like that old proverb, "For want of a nail, the battle was lost." The big rules are easy to follow. It's the little ones that often get ignored and end up biting you on the rear.

And of course, this is your game. If you don't want to follow a particular rule, and everyone else at the table agrees, then you don't have to bother with it. But just remember that poker rules were developed for a reason. The rules and procedures in this chapter are standard, and they're recommended. Apply them or not as you see fit.

How to Handle Cards During Play

It's bad form to lift cards completely off the table (don't hold them close to your chest, and so forth), and it's entirely against the rules to remove them from the table or conceal them in any way.

Tip

It's perfectly okay to look at your cards more than once, but handling them too much has some drawbacks. You may inadvertently foul your hand, and frequent glances can sometimes help your opponents guess what you're holding.

Here's a good way to look at your cards: Square them. Hold your hands over one end of the cards and use one thumb to gently squeeze up the corners, showing the indices.

Put a short stack of chips on the cards when you're finished. This prevents the dealer from accidentally **mucking** your hand (retrieving the cards and tossing them into the discard pile). It happens more often than you might think. Unprotected cards are permanently dead when they hit the muck. Even if the dealer made a mistake, there is no way to resuscitate that hand. Remember, it's your responsibility to **protect your hand** and prevent it from being **fouled** (made invalid).

There are other ways that a hand can be fouled: when two hands touch or are otherwise intermingled, when cards fall off the table, or when a player accidentally mucks cards.

Let's say you're in a four-way showdown and an opponent announces that she has a straight. You muck a pair of kings. Another player mucks. A third player turns over a pair of queens. The last player proudly turns up a worthless hand that at first glance looks like a straight. Everyone stares at the two hands for a long moment and then the dealer announces that the queens win. The owner of the busted straight is surprised, and then realizes that she misread her hand.

Yes, it was an honest mistake, but it's too late. You mucked the kings, and your hand is dead. The pot goes to the pair of queens.

The Cards Speak

The previous scenario is the perfect reason why it's a bad idea to muck a hand in a showdown unless you're absolutely sure it's a loser. If you have any possibility of winning, it's better to expose the cards and allow everyone at the table to determine the winner. The rule is that **the cards speak.** In other words, verbal announcements are invalid and unnecessary; the only thing that matters is what can be seen on the cards.

Some people don't like to reveal losing hands in a showdown. They're embarrassed or they don't want to give away information about the hand they played, so they just muck. That's acceptable if a hand is clearly **busted** (worthless rags), but I've seen many hands where the supposed winner wasn't. Here's a typical example in hold 'em:

You hold:

Your opponent has:

And the board shows:

At the showdown your opponent triumphantly flips over his hand and exclaims, "I've got the high two pair." Does that beat a pair of jacks? Yes, it does. Should you muck? No, because your hand isn't a pair. It's two pairs: jacks and fives. You're the winner.

So when the showdown comes, don't be coy, and don't hesitate. Just reveal your cards. Announce the hand if it pleases you, but the cards speak.

Shuffling and Dealing

In private poker games, everyone deals once in every round. There are some practical reasons for this. First, it's fair that everyone equally share the chore of distributing cards. Also, if everyone deals, then nobody controls the cards exclusively. This reduces the chance of systematic cheating. And finally, everyone gets to handle the cards, so (theoretically at least) an altered deck will be quickly discovered.

THE FACT IS...

Players are not required to reveal their hands if everyone folds to one player before a showdown. But if anyone mucks at a showdown, any player at the table can request to see the mucked hand. The purpose of this rule is to prevent collusion, but it should be invoked sparingly because it may offend some opponents.

Some poker games have one person who deals, and that's okay if everyone trusts the dealer. In these situations, the dealer position (called the **button** or puck) still moves clockwise around the table. A plastic disk or some other handy item is used to designate the rotating dealer; this designation determines the blinds and the order of action.

As I mentioned previously, this is your game. So you can shuffle and deal in whatever way you choose as long as the table is in agreement. But, obviously, it's better if the cards are thoroughly mixed and properly distributed. This makes disputes less likely, and it helps to prevent cheating.

Here's how shuffling is done in a casino. It's the recommended procedure. Follow it as you see fit.

Shuffling, Step 1: The Scramble

First you scramble the cards. Simply spread them out face down on the table and swirl them around with both hands. Use a circular motion. There is intentionally no pattern or control of where the cards go. Some will go sideways, some will move with your hands, others will be caught underneath the pile and will stay in one place.

Scramble the cards well for about five or ten seconds, until they're just a big messy heap. Wheeeee! Then gently lift up the pile so the backs are facing you, and square the cards against the table. Players at the table will be able to see all the faces of the cards (in a blur) as you shift the cards into a pack.

Now put the pack face down on the table. It's important that you keep the faces of the cards down close to the table through the rest of the shuffle. Your hands should always be above the deck, not below it. Don't put cards in your hand (resting in your palm) until you're ready to deal.

Shuffling, Step 2: The Riffle

This is the classic shuffle that most people remember from childhood games of rummy and old maid. But, of course, we'll do it more efficiently for our poker game.

Lift off the top half of the deck and place it at the end of the bottom half.

Square each half with one hand and then use your thumbs to bend up the inside corners of each stack (the corners that are closest to you). Riffle/mingle them together so that the inside corners of the cards from the two stacks are layered one over another. Then push and slide the two halves together until all the cards are back into one stack. Don't tip up the cards too much when you're shuffling!

Riffle-shuffle once again, then square the deck.

Shuffling, Step 3: The Overhand

Now use one hand to hold the deck from above. Use the other hand to pull off (lengthwise) a clump of cards, five or ten. Lay the clump next to the deck and do it again, putting each new clump on top of the previous clump. Keep going until you've transferred all the cards to a new pile.

Shuffling, Step 4: The Finish

Riffle-shuffle once more. Then cut the cards (lift off the top half of the deck, place it on the table, and put the bottom half on top). In home games, the player to the dealer's right can be the person who cuts the deck.

Square the deck after the cut, and you're ready to deal.

So it's scramble, riffle, riffle, overhand, riffle, cut. The whole process should take less than forty seconds once you've got the hang of it (casino dealers do it even faster).

In casinos, after the cut, the dealer will put the deck over a plastic card, and hold the deck and the plastic card when dealing. This prevents the dealer from taking cards from the bottom of the deck. If you have a plastic deck-size card, use it.

Dealing: Before the Flop

The first card goes to the player on your left. Then every player gets one card in turn, and then one for yourself. Repeat the process until everyone has the required number of cards.

Tip

Dealers in casinos usually announce the number of players in a hand after the round is finished. You don't have to do this in a home game, but an announcement does help players keep track of the action and who is in the hand.

There's a whole science to "pitching cards" that I won't go into here. Just remember to deliver the cards in a way that keeps them from being exposed. There are various rules for handling cards when they're accidentally exposed. Sometimes the hand is declared dead, in other cases the card is shown to the table and becomes a burn card. We'll cover those cases in Chapter 10.

As players surrender cards, collect the face-down cards into a pile (the muck) near your position. When everyone has finished betting or folding, sweep all the bets into the center of the table (the pot).

Dealing: The Flop and Afterwards

Pull a card off the top of the deck, face down. Slide it under the chips in the pot. This is the burn card.

Deal out three cards face down. Turn them over and spread them out in a line. This is the flop.

As before, pull cards into the muck as players surrender hands, then sweep bets into the center of the table when everyone has finished betting or folding.

Burn a card (put it face down under the chips), then deal out one card and turn it over. Put it next to the other three exposed cards. This is the turn.

Collect folded hands. Sweep bets into the pot. Burn a card, and then deal the last card. This is the river.

When the hand is over, square all the cards and pass them to the player on your left.

THE FACT IS...

After the river has been dealt, a dealer sometimes will count the remaining cards in the deck (usually during a pause while a player is considering action). The purpose is to insure that cards are not missing. With seven players (two cards each), five cards on the board, and three burn cards, you should have thirty cards left in the deck. Six players leaves thirty-two, and so on.

Splashing the Pot and Other Taboos

It's somewhat ironic that nearly every dramatic betting maneuver you've seen in the movies is forbidden in real poker.

Splashing the Pot

Throwing chips into the pot is called splashing the pot. This is forbidden because the dealer and other players must be able to verify that a bettor has contributed the correct amount. The dealer must count down the chips in the pot if it has been splashed. This is time consuming and a real drag. The correct way to bet is to place chips in front of your position, so that everyone can see the bet. In some games, you then push the chips into the pot. In other games, the dealer will collect the chips in front of you at the end of the betting round and put them in the pot.

String Bets

You've probably seen this in the movies. The hero bets $1,000. Then the bad guy says, "I call your $1,000 [dramatic pause], and raise you $10,000."

Scary, huh? That's called a string bet or string raise, and it's not allowed (except in the movies). When a player says, "Call," then that's it. No raise is permitted. This rule prevents a bettor from using a call as a psychological ploy to read an opponent's reaction, then switching the call into a raise when weakness is perceived.

 **Tip**

If you don't have the proper denomination chip for a particular bet or raise, just state your intention and put out a larger chip (or chips). The dealer (or you) can make change at the end of the round. If you don't make a verbal declaration, a larger chip usually will be considered a call unless it's close to or exactly the denomination of a raise.

Another type of string bet is to say nothing, put enough chips out for a call, and then return to the stack to raise. Once again, this is forbidden. Some people do it innocently because they're just counting chips, but it's still against the rules. If an opponent objects, the wager will be restricted to a call.

The best way to avoid any confusion is to simply say, "Raise." That's binding, then you can take as much time as is required to get the chips off your stack.

Acting Out of Turn

Consider the hand I described in Chapter 2, when Sandy won over Erin. What would have happened before the flop if Luke had announced out of turn, "I'm raising this one"? It's probable that Mickey would have folded rather than calling, and the betting might not have been capped in the first round. At the very least it would have cost Sandy $3 and possibly more.

Acting out of turn is unfair, and it disrupts the game. Players should always wait until the action reaches them before tossing cards, checking, raising, or calling.

Sharing Hands and Revealing Cards

This is a taboo related to the previous one. It's against the rules for someone with a live hand to reveal those cards to another active player (unless everyone else has folded). Anyone who does this is cheating.

Some players bend this rule by showing cards to others at the table who have folded. Revealing cards in this manner is bad form, but it's acceptable as long as the other person doesn't comment or offer advice. To do so violates the principle of one player to a hand. Also, when cards are revealed in this way, then you have the right to see those cards when the hand is over. This rule is called show one, show all, and it insures that everyone has equal access to the same game information.

In some games, you'll hear players loudly speculating on other people's hands. "Uh-oh! A pair is on the board. Josh has a full house." This is bad manners at best and borderline cheating at worst (it may unfairly help someone). Ditto for people who talk about hands that they've folded.

Of course, you may profit more in some situations by allowing minor infractions to pass. It's a judgment call with many variables. Forcing a strict interpretation of the rules may put an opponent on guard and make him play better. You don't want that.

Tapping the Table While Thinking

There are two ways to check; a player can say, "Check," or he can tap the table. A person who unconsciously taps the table while thinking may be restricted to a check if other players subsequently take action. At the very least, idle tapping often causes unpleasant confusion. Other players bet or check, the thinker usually doesn't notice at first, and then he finally complains when it's too late. The whole thing can quickly become a comedy of errors. So be aware that tapping means a check.

Pulling the Pot Too Soon

You'll avoid a lot of problems if you wait until all the cards have been revealed and everyone has conceded before grabbing at the pot. Unfortunately, some players like to slow roll as a form of psychological warfare. They wait quietly until you're reaching for the pot before they reveal a winning hand. By that time your cards may have gone into the muck. So guess who gets the pot?

In casinos, this problem is solved by prohibiting players from pulling the pot. The casino dealer pushes the pot to the winner. That rule is a bit much for most home games, but use it if you find yourself having problems with disputes or slow rollers.

Table Stakes

When I was a wee lad I would watch poker movies and think about strategy. Back then it seemed pretty straightforward; the person with the most money would simply bet more than opponents could afford to call. Competitors would thus be forced out of the pot. Invariably, someone would fold a killer hand because he had no money to back it up. The hapless loser would moan piteously, "Ah cain't call that bet without sellin' the homestead."

I promised myself to always sit down at a poker table with one million dollars, and that would insure my income forever. I never did figure out why anyone other than a millionaire would sit in a game like that, and it never occurred to me that someone with ten million might wipe me out.

Ahhhh, the movies.

In the real world of poker, you cannot be forced out of a pot when you run out of money. The game uses a system called table stakes to prevent this. The chips (or cash) sitting in front of a player at the beginning of a hand is the only money that can be used in the hand. If a player runs out of money, this is called being all in. If two players are left, and one is all in, the hand is completed with no more betting. If three or more players are left, the subsequent bets go into a side pot. The player who is all in can win the main pot, and someone else can win the side pot. Or another player can win both pots. But the all-in player can't win any of the later bets.

And that's the negative side of table stakes. You can't pull out your checkbook and raise if you smack a monster hand. So it's always a good idea to have an ample supply of money sitting in front of you.

When a player does go all in, the side pot is settled first, at the showdown, and then the main pot is decided.

 **Tip**

The table stakes rule can be suspended if everyone in the hand agrees to it, but beware. If someone wants to raise the bet dramatically, and someone is willing to call, then at least one player is surely being suckered in some way.

Dealer's Choice, Wild Cards, and Betting Limits

Dealers traditionally get to choose the poker version that they will be dealing. In a private game it is not unusual to play four or five different types of poker randomly in the course of an evening. Dealers usually want to play whatever version they feel is their strongest.

But as with everything else in a home game, this can be modified as the group chooses. You can play just hold 'em, just seven-card stud, just hold 'em and five-card draw, fifteen different versions, or whatever.

Similarly, wild cards (cards that can be used for any rank or suit) are another choice that is traditionally a right of the dealer. Wild cards can be jokers, one-eyed jacks, deuces, the queen of spades, just about anything.

If you decide to play with wild cards, keep in mind that they add an extra element of chance and gambling to the game. Let's say you have:

And the board shows:

You have jacks full of tens and the only card that can beat you is 9♣ (to make a straight flush). Under normal circumstances, that's just one card out of fifty-two. But if deuces are wild, the probability of losing has increased from one chance to five.

Besides choosing the poker version and wild cards, dealers also get to choose betting limits (if the table agrees). We'll cover the political side of betting limits later. Right now just remember that you don't have to play every hand. Just throw your cards away or ask to be dealt out if the stakes for a particular game are too expensive.

Essentially

♠ It's your responsibility to protect your hand and prevent it from being fouled. One way to do this is to put a short stack of chips on your cards to prevent them from being accidentally mucked by the dealer.

♥ Don't muck your hand in a showdown unless you're absolutely certain that it's a loser. The rule is that the cards speak; don't rely on verbal declarations.

♦ Dealing is an important part of the game. Disputes are less likely when the cards are thoroughly mixed and properly distributed.

♣ A casino-quality shuffle includes a scramble, riffle, riffle, overhand shuffle, riffle, and cut, in that order.

♠ Poker rules prohibit splashing the pot, string bets, and acting out of turn.

♥ Adding money to your stake during a hand is not allowed. You can only play with table stakes, the money you have available at the start of the hand.

THE FACT IS...

Wild cards can be fun, but they add an element of chance that makes strategy less effective. If you're a good player, you'll have a bigger advantage over opponents when you play without wild cards.

PART TWO

Strategies for Hold 'Em

CHAPTER 4

Starting Hands and Position

Remember the lottery example back in Chapter 1? You could buy the first two numbers of a lottery ticket for a penny. Would you continue with that ticket if the numbers were duds? No, you'd throw it away and start fresh. Dud numbers lower your chances of winning a prize.

The same principle applies to hold 'em starting cards (indeed, it goes for all poker starting cards). A low-quality combination at the beginning of a hand reduces your chances of winning the pot. Of course, anything *can* happen. You could play something that seems worthless, such as 7♦ 2♠, and still flop 7♥ 7♣ 7♠. But results like that are infrequent. Over time, 7♦ 2♠ will be beaten consistently by hands such as A♠ K♠ and J♥ T♥. Some starting card combinations perform better than others. It's just that simple.

In fact, hand selection is easily the single most important factor that separates players who are consistent winners from those who are long-term losers.

A Good Starting Hand Has...

Starting hands are like everything else in poker, very situational. Your position in relation to the dealer, the number of active players, the number of bets or raises ahead of you, and the possibility of bets or raises behind you all have an enormous impact on the viability of any particular combination of cards.

So the "good" attributes listed on the next few pages are only the first standards for judging a hand. In other words, a hand with some good qualities is not necessarily always playable. More importantly, any hand that doesn't meet these basic standards can be immediately folded.

THE FACT IS...

Most of the profit in poker does not come from bluffing or other trickery. Profit mainly comes from capitalizing on the mistakes that other people make. Your goal is to make zero mistakes and to seek out opponents who are unskilled and/or likely to make poor strategic choices.

And remember, we're talking about hold 'em in these chapters. Similar standards generally apply to other poker versions in most circumstances, but a game such as razz or lowball (see Chapter 10) would obviously be very different.

A note about notation:

Lowercase *s* after a card combination (**AKs**, **T9s**, etc.) indicates the cards are of the same suit.

Lowercase *n* after a card combination (**QJn**, **98n**, etc.) indicates the cards are not of the same suit.

Card combinations without an *s* or *n* can be either suited or not suited.

T stands for ten.

First we'll cover desirable hand attributes, and then we'll group the hands into ranks of relative value.

Big Cards

Let's say you hold **AK** and your opponent holds **98** before the flop. It's a curious truth that you both have an exactly equal chance of finishing the hand with a pair, two pairs, trips, a full house, or quads (four of a kind). But in a heads-up situation (only these two hands in competition), **AK** has a tremendous advantage because it will win if **98** does not improve to at least a pair. And **AK** will win if both hands improve equally. Consider a board showing the following:

AK was beating **98** before the flop and on the flop, then lost the lead on the turn, but regained it on the river. Both players finished with two pairs, but **AK** finished with aces and fives, while **98** dragged in with nines and eights. So, big cards are good. Two cards that are jacks or higher always deserve a second look (though they're not necessarily always playable).

Suited Cards

Two cards of the same suit are more likely to make a flush than two cards of mixed suits. Suited cards flop a four-card flush about 11 percent of the time. When that happens, the probability of finishing with a flush is better than 1 in 3 (2:1). Suited cards always deserve a second look, but only long enough to determine if they have additional good attributes. Suit alone is not enough to play a starting hand.

Connectors

Cards that are next to each other in rank have a higher probability of making a straight. This probability drops dramatically as the gap between the cards increases. **JT** can make a straight four ways (**AKQ**, **KQ9**, **Q98**, **987**), while **J7** can only make a straight with **T98**. As with suited cards, connectors alone are not good enough to play a starting hand, but it's an attribute you should consider.

Pairs

A pocket pair is generally a good thing. Of course, **AA** is worth much more than 33, but any pair should get a second look.

Pairs are typically divided into three groups that reflect their relative power and profitability. Big pairs are **AA** through **JJ**. Medium pairs are **TT** through **77**. Small pairs are **66** and below.

A Word About Tens

Tens are a strange breed in the hold 'em world. They're not really big cards, but they can often carry a hand like a big card. For example, **TT** is closer in strength to **JJ** than to **99**.

And a ten is required for any high straight, so **JT** is often as powerful as **QJ**. The thing to remember about tens is their chameleon-like quality. They can be valuable, but they should be played carefully, especially when they're in gapped hands.

Ranking the Starting Hands

The following ranks are general, and there is a range of value within each rank. Keep in mind that a hand's value can change dramatically on the flop. Nevertheless, a premium hand like **AA** will consistently earn more money than a bargain hand like **76s**. Also remember that the suited version of a hand is always *much* stronger than the mixed-suit version.

Hold 'Em Starting Hands

Premium hands	AA, KK, QQ, JJ, AK
Average hands	AQ, AJ, KQ, KJ, QJ, JT, AT, TT, 99, 88
Bargain hands	**T9s** and suited connectors down to **54s**
	77 and pairs below
	Axs (suited hands containing an ace and any small card)
	KTs, QTs, J9s
Trash	Any hand that doesn't appear in the above three groups

Hands without an *s* or *n* indicate both suited and non-suited.

Heads-up Comparisons

Premium hands are the most reliable and profitable combinations. Big pairs can frequently pick up the pot without improvement, and a single ace or king on the board will often put **AK** over the top.

In contrast, average hands are generally less reliable and less profitable. They usually need improvement, and they're often beaten by premium hands.

Bargain hands continue the downward trend in quality. They almost always need improvement, and they sometimes lose even when the board gives them a big boost. Nevertheless, they're still profitable when played carefully.

Trash hands fall right off the scale of profitability. They almost always cost money over the long term regardless of how well they are played. One example would be **65n**. That combination would be buried against premium and average hands like **QQ**, **AK**, and **KJ** if the flop were unexceptional (**QT7** or **JT4**).

Note that some poker authors divide hold 'em starting hands into as many as eight categories plus trash. This is because there is a big difference between a nearly premium combination like **AQs** and something much closer to the bargain end like **ATn**. While this distinction is very important, I decided not to cross your eyes with a list that has more than half a dozen categories and six dozen entries. Clearly, **AQs** is superior to **QJn**, **KQs** is stronger than **JTn**, and **AA** has an advantage over **AKn**.

Tip

Some hands are "borderline trash" like **K9s**, **Q9s**, **J8s**, and **T9n**. It's not necessarily always incorrect to play them, and you'll sometimes see a good player throw in borderline hands to mix up opponents, but it's a judgment call. These hands are frequently more trouble than they're worth. Beginners should avoid them.

The more you play hold 'em, the more you'll learn the subtle nuances of these combinations, and you'll see that every hand really deserves its own category (see Chapter 6).

Big Pairs and the Game of Life

Poker has many similarities to the larger game of life, and the relative strength of big pairs in hold 'em is one example. Big pairs push other hands around. They dominate the game. But big pairs have an interesting weakness. They're more likely to lose when there are many players in the pot. The probability of someone hitting a long-shot hand goes up when there are eight or nine contestants rather than two or three; so it's like the little guys piling on to defeat the bully. In contrast, suited hands and connectors *tend to do well* against multiple competitors. These hands win less frequently, but when they hit against a full table, it's often for a monster pot.

Tempting Trash and Going "On-Tilt"

Sometimes you'll see people win with Kx, Jx, T3s, 76n, and other garbage. If you play hold 'em a lot, you'll occasionally be beaten silly by these hands. Here's a typical scenario. You hold A♥ K♥ and your opponent has 6♣ 5♥. The board shows:

You flopped a four-flush and top pair. The turn improved you to two pairs. Meanwhile, your opponent played trash. She went for a gutshot straight draw (needed one specific rank), and she made it on the river. Ouch! It happens.

Losing a pile o' chips can seriously mess with your attitude and put you on-tilt. You may be tempted to play loose and crazy like the person who beat you. If you give in to this temptation you'll soon be beaten by a good hand (probably by the same person who beat you with a bad one), and that will mess with your attitude even more.

I've seen players get so psychologically distressed that they abandon all pretext of using strategy. They simply play everything. Of course, these "steamrollers" (or steamers) inevitably lose all their money. And then they blame it on bad luck! Remember, any two cards *can* win. But trash probably won't.

Position Is Power

Now that you know more about starting hands, let's go back to the round I described in Chapter 2. You'll recall that I said Mickey played his hand poorly. Here are all the hands:

Seat 1, Mickey: Called 6♦ 5♦

Seat 2, Sandy: Raised A♣ K♣

Seat 3, Luke: Raised J♥ J♦

Seat 4, Jasmine: Folded 8♠ 4♠

Seat 5, Colin (dealer/button): Folded T♥ 9♣

Seat 6, Chris (little blind): Folded Q♦ T♥

Seat 7, Erin (big blind): Raised A♥ A♠

As you can see, Mickey called the big blind. Sandy raised, and Luke reraised. Seats four and five folded, and Erin capped it. Then Mickey folded. He lost $3 without seeing the flop.

Let's take Mickey out of seat one and put him on the button (last to act before the blinds). How would he play **65s** facing two raises? Do you think Mickey would muck his cards and save some money? Yes, he probably would.

Okay, let's put Mickey back into seat one, and swap Erin (**AA**) with Luke (**JJ**). Erin makes the second raise behind Sandy (**AKs**). What would Luke do? Would he be thinking about the cards that Erin and Sandy are holding? Yes, Luke would correctly suspect that at least one of the raisers (if not both of them) might have a pair that would beat two jacks. He would probably call rather than raise. And he might even muck the jacks if he's got a good "read" on Erin and Sandy.

The lesson here is that position is power. The later you act, the more information you have about your opponents. In fact, all hold 'em strategies vary in direct relation to a player's position (it's like Einstein's Theory of Relativity applied to poker).

Early position is generally defined as the first two (or three) seats to act. Middle position would be the next three seats, and late position would be the remaining seats.

Premium hands can be played in any position, but they're particularly well suited for raising in early position.

Average hands also can be played in any position if the game conditions are right. That's a big "if" that we'll cover later, but average hands are generally better suited to middle position and late position in a pot that hasn't been too aggressively raised.

Bargain hands are best suited for late position in an unraised pot. This insures that a bargain hand will get enough action to be profitable if the flop is a good one.

We'll expand the previous three paragraphs into a detailed pre-flop strategy in Chapter 6, but first we're going to cover poker economics and the general effects of folding, calling, and raising.

In the meantime, just remember that Mickey played a bargain hand in early position, and it cost him one bet. Ultimately, his fold was correct, but he misread the aggressiveness of the table. Also, Sandy and Erin noticed Mickey's call and then fold. Both made a mental note to use that information later in the game.

Essentially

♠ The best hold 'em starting hands include big cards, suited cards, connectors, or pairs. It usually takes two or three of these attributes to make a playable starting hand.

♥ Trash hands may look tempting, but they invariably cost more money than they win.

♦ An unexpected loss can cause some players to go "on-tilt" and abandon strategy. It's an understandable reaction, but losses will get worse when a person plays every hand, or plays too aggressively.

♣ Position is power in hold 'em. Players who are closer to the button have more information about their opponents.

♠ Some starting hands are most profitable in early position, and some are best played in late position.

CHAPTER 5

Poker Economics

People who are familiar with blackjack and video poker sometimes get frustrated when they play games such as hold 'em or seven-card stud. The typical complaint goes something like this:

"I have exactly seven cards. I can't replace any of my cards, and my opponents can see most of my hand. The only real decisions are bet, raise, or fold. Where's the control? Where's the strategy?"

Essentially, these people wish that they could somehow "hit" the hand, as in blackjack. Or they want to draw to improve it, as in video poker. They're stuck thinking of strategy as something to "use" on the implements of the game (the cards). But genuine poker is more Zen-like. Poker strategy is about having a superior understanding of the relative strength of hands in their current and possibly future form. This knowledge allows you to compete when you have an advantage, and it gives you the ability to disappear like a ninja when your opponent is poised to strike. It's martial arts with cards. Your power is exercised through the outwardly simple tools of checking or betting, and folding, calling, or raising.

The Power of Folding

Imagine if you sat in a 3-6 hold 'em game for four hours, and you did nothing but fold. You'd lose about $15 per hour in blind bets, or $60 during the session.

That's roughly comparable to what Sandy won on just one pot (in our Chapter 2 example).

Now imagine if you played like Mickey and called every hand. That would cost about $80 per hour, or $320 during a session, and that's just one call and no raises before the flop. The cost goes up with every raise and every round. Mickey has to win a lot more chips to cover the price of not folding.

THE FACT IS...

Royal flushes tend to win small pots in games such as hold 'em and seven-card stud because opponents can plainly see suited high cards on the board. Even an opponent with a straight flush would tend to play his hand cautiously against three suited high cards.

Muhammad Ali said, "Float like a butterfly, and sting like a bee." The poker equivalent of this philosophy is to be tight and aggressive. Your opponents should be swinging at air most of the time. Remember, every player has an equal probability of being dealt the best hand. The only way for you to create an imbalance in your favor is to spend little or nothing on losing hands, and cause your opponents to contribute a lot when your hand is a winner.

So folding has more power than most people realize. Let's say your opponent has the strongest possible hand, a royal flush. What happens when you fold? Your opponent's royal flush loses some of its worth. If everyone folds then a royal flush is essentially worthless (winning only the blinds or antes).

Fortunately for us, most players don't fold, or they fold later than they should, and thus it is the weaker hands that give the stronger ones value. Or to put it another way, the value of a hand is only partially determined by its actual strength. The other *huge* factor is how many people are competing for the pot.

A game with nine opponents plays differently than a game with six opponents. And when games become shorthanded, with five or fewer opponents, then strategies become radically different.

So at this point let's establish the parameters of a "standard game" and explore strategies for beating the standard. Then later we'll discuss tactics for non-standard games.

A standard home game would have five to seven opponents. Let's say six opponents on average. Four or fewer would be a short game. Eight to ten opponents would be a big game. For the sake of consistency with previous examples, we'll say the limits are $3–$6, but they could easily be $30–$60 or $500–$1,000.

Of course, the opponents in our game (their motivations to bet, call, fold, and so forth) are important in determining our strategies, and we'll talk more about opponents at the end of this chapter.

Pot Odds and Betting Decisions

Here's a quiz. You hold Q♣ J♠ in late position and the flop comes 9♦ 8♥ 4♠. That gives you a gutshot draw to a high straight. Should you call a bet on the flop or fold?

What is your answer?

Your answer should be that I haven't given you enough information to make an informed decision. I haven't told you how much money is in the pot or the size of the bet. The two figures together are used to calculate **pot odds**, a system that helps you decide if a hand is worth pursuing.

Essentially, it's a refined version of saying, "Hey, this bet is too expensive." Or in some circumstances, "What a bargain!"

The calculation is simple. A player compares the money in the pot to the proposed bet. For example, $18 in the pot and

$3 to call means the pot is six times larger than the bet. The pot odds are 6:1 (or some people say the pot is "offering" 6:1).

Sounds great, but what are the chances of actually winning that money? If the odds *against* the hand (essentially the probability of losing) are higher than 6:1, the hand should be folded. Why? Because in the long run the hand will not earn enough to justify the cost of the competition.

Let's say the pot odds are 6:1 and the odds against the hand are 11:1. That means the player will win $6 once (on average) and lose $1 eleven times. The deficit is $5. Not good. Roulette would be a cheaper game.

THE FACT IS...

Casinos use a system that is similar to pot odds when they set the rules for their games. For example, the odds against an "outside" red/black bet winning (from a player's perspective) are 20:18. But the casino is paying only 18:18, or 1:1. So it's a bad bet for players, and a good bet for the casino.

But if the pot odds are reversed, 11:1 in the pot and only 6:1 against the hand, the player will win $11 once and lose $1 six times. That's a positive gain of $5. The hand should be played.

Of course, there's no way to predict exactly when that one win will occur, but it doesn't matter. It's like owning a slot machine. The individual spins aren't as important as the long-term favorable odds.

Pot Odds Made Easy

But how can you know the exact odds against a hand? In most cases you can't know exactly, but you can estimate very easily. Here's a classic example. You hold:

And the board shows:

This is a no-brainer. You have fifteen outs (cards in the deck that will complete the hand). Eight cards in the deck will give you a straight, and nine cards will give you a flush. Two of those cards are the same (giving you a straight flush), so the total is fifteen rather than seventeen.

A four-card flush always has nine outs. An open-ended four-card straight (four adjacent ranks) has eight outs. Gutshot straights have four outs. Two pairs to a full house is four outs. Pairs to trips is two outs.

The next two tables give you the probability and odds against improving on the flop and after the flop.

Probability of Improving on the Flop

Hand	Improvement	Probability	Odds Against
Any two cards	Making a pair	32.4%	2:1
Suited	Four-flush	10.9%	8:1
Pocket pair	Trips	11.8%	7.5:1

Probability of Improving After the Flop

Outs	Probability	Odds	Outs	Probability	Odds
1	4.3%	22.5:1	9	35.0%	2:1
2	8.4%	11:1	10	38.4%	1.5:1
3	12.5%	7:1	11	41.7%	1.5:1
4	16.5%	5:1	12	45.0%	1.25:1
5	20.4%	4:1	13	48.1%	1:1
6	24.1%	3:1	14	51.2%	1:1
7	27.8%	2.5:1	15	54.1%	1:1
8	31.5%	2:1	16	57.0%	0.75:1

Odds against are rounded. Probability of improving after the flop is with two cards to come (turn and river).

One easy way to calculate the probability of improving without memorizing the table is to simply multiply the outs by four, and then put a percent sign behind the result. That will get you close to the real number.

Another way is to just learn the odds for the most common hands. An open-ended draw to a straight flush is better than 1:1. Four-card straights and four-card flushes are about 2:1. Two pairs to a full house is 5:1, and one pair to trips is 11:1 (after the flop).

Okay, let's consider the hand in the most recent example, Q♦ J♦ with a board of A♠ T♦ 9♦. The pot holds $54 and the price of a call is $3. Is this a good bet?

Yes, it is. The pot is offering a hefty 18:1, and the odds of making a straight or flush are about 1:1. You have a tremendous edge. This hand is worth a raise (but we'll get to raises in a later section).

Pot Odds Made Even Easier

Here's a way to make pot odds even easier to calculate (in case you really hate math). You don't have to know the exact amount of money in the pot. Just guess. Look in the center of the table and make a reasonable estimate, then compare it to the bet you're considering. Those are the pot odds.

Now, let's go back to the original question of the inside straight. You hold QJ in late position and the flop comes 984 rainbow (mixed suits). The pot has $24 and it will cost $6 to call a raise. What should you do?

The pot is offering 4:1; the odds against the straight are 5:1. This is a hand you should toss.

But what if the pot has $51 and the cost of a call is only $3? Now the pot odds are 17:1. So a call would be correct.

As a general rule, big pots make it easy for drawing hands (hands that need improvement) to justify sticking around. Smaller pots aren't worth the risk. Think about how that affects the big pairs vs. bargain hand effect that I described in the previous chapter. An enormous pot with a cheap price for entry is not what a big pair wants to see.

In fact, some very unlikely hands become playable if the pot odds are large enough.

Implied Pot Odds

Let's say you're on the button with **66**. Four players call ahead of you. The pot is offering 5.5:1 (including the blinds). The chance of flopping trips is 7.5:1. This would seem to indicate a fold, but remember that you'll likely win bets in later rounds if you flop a six. The value of those extra expected bets should be included when you decide to call or fold before the flop.

Tip

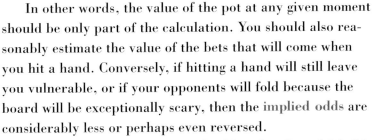

Sometimes people continue playing hands that have turned into losers because they've invested a lot of money in the pot. This is a mistake. The only calculation that matters is the total value of the pot compared to the actual chance of hitting the hand. A bad hand cannot be "healed" by a big pot.

In other words, the value of the pot at any given moment should be only part of the calculation. You should also reasonably estimate the value of the bets that will come when you hit a hand. Conversely, if hitting a hand will still leave you vulnerable, or if your opponents will fold because the board will be exceptionally scary, then the implied odds are considerably less or perhaps even reversed.

An example of this would be **9♠ 8♠** with a flop of **A♣ Q♦ J♠**. A **T♣** on the turn wouldn't necessarily be a good thing. It would give you a queen-high straight, but it would also fill in an ace-high straight for anyone holding a king.

Another example, somewhat more complex, is the straight-flush draw I described earlier. You have **Q♦ J♦** and the board shows **A♠ T♦ 9♦**. Obviously, **K♦** or **8♦** on the turn or river would be ideal, but any king or eight would likely win the hand. Ironically, a diamond other than king or eight could be trouble. It would fill in your flush, but someone with **A♦** and another diamond would have a higher flush.

Tip

Drawing to a four-flush or an open-ended four-card straight generally requires a large pot and at least two opponents (preferably more than two) on the flop and turn, because the odds against making the hand are 2:1. One win must exceed the price of two losses for the play to be profitable.

Calling vs. Raising

Moe is a friend of mine and a great guy, but he's a really bad poker player. No matter how much advice I give him, he has no patience for the intricacies of the game. Moe once complained, "Everyone always folds when I raise with a good hand."

It never occurred to him that raising isn't just a way to build the pot and win more money; it's also a powerful tool for changing the pot odds, thus making some hands unprofitable to play. Moe doesn't want to think about pot odds because, he says, "It hurts my head." He just wants to win hands.

Loose and Passive

Poor Moe. He wins plenty of hands, but his pots are usually small. Moe is loose (frequently willing to put money in the pot), and he's passive (only bets and raises with extremely strong hands). In Moe's mind this "conservative" approach saves money when hands go bad; the savings supposedly allow him to play more hands and win more pots. But this thinking is all wrong. Loose and passive is a style of play that builds pots for other people. A guy like Moe is a calling station, the type of player who will call to "keep you honest" even when you're obviously holding a superior hand. Moe is an ideal opponent. Playing against him is like playing poker with an ATM. He just keeps spitting out cash.

Loose and Aggressive

Jay will sometimes raise without even looking at his cards. Yes, some people actually do this. I suppose they think it's exciting. This style of play is loose and aggressive. Players like Jay are very dangerous because they're difficult to read. Jay might raise with trash or with a premium hand. Who knows? He's not stupid, but he's reckless. Jay will...not... fold unless he's absolutely sure that he's beaten, and he'll enthusiastically build a pot while hoping to catch a miracle. Sometimes it happens; a lot of times it doesn't. Jay is not a long-term winner, but he tends to magnify the money shifts at a table, and he alters pot odds in ways that are not always beneficial to advantage players. Going heads-up with Jay can be profitable, but he's not an ideal opponent.

Tight and Passive

Mickey is the exact opposite of Jay. He doesn't play a lot of hands, and he rarely raises. He's the sort of person who dis- appears when Jay comes charging into a pot. Players like Mickey are tight and passive. They're sometimes called rocks. Mickey doesn't lose a lot, and he doesn't win a lot. He's very predictable, very beatable, but not a source of big profit for advantage players.

Tight and Aggressive

Sandy, Erin, and Luke are all tight and aggressive. They're nearly as unpredictable and dangerous as Jay when they're in a hand because they frequently raise rather than just call. But they're also like Mickey, difficult to pin down. They check when opponents expect them to bet, and they fold when others are hoping for a call or raise.

There is no way to absolutely predict what a tight and aggressive player will do because the cards, the pot, and the other players are creating a per-hand strategy that is con- stantly adjusting to the immediate situation. Tight and aggressive players can be a lot of fun to watch, but a real challenge to beat.

Through the Looking Glass

In Lewis Carroll's *Through the Looking-Glass* everything looks very normal and correct when Alice views her room from one side of the mirror. Then she steps through the glass and looks beyond the original boundaries of the room. That's when things become very strange. Sometimes she has to walk backwards to go forward, but other times her feet work in the normal way.

From a metaphorical point of view, the first four chapters of this book were a close-up view of the mirror. You were looking at your reflection in the game. Everything was relatively simple and straightforward. But in this chapter you have stepped through the looking glass. Suddenly, things are different, and much more flexible. Betting or raising can have a variety of effects depending on the situation. Raising with a premium hand is generally correct, but not always. Raising with an apparently marginal hand isn't necessarily wrong (especially if your opponent is Mickey). Everything is situational. The math *always* works, but it works differently as the mix of opponents changes.

This is an important concept. Keep it in mind as we cover betting and raising strategies in the next chapter.

"I don't think they play at all fairly, and they all quarrel so dreadfully one can't hear oneself speak—and they don't seem to have any rules in particular; at least, if there are, nobody attends to them—and you've no idea how confusing it is all the things being alive."

—Alice, in *Alice's Adventures in Wonderland*, by Lewis Carroll

Essentially

♠ Folding is a powerful strategy for minimizing losses. An opponent's strong hand loses some of its value when you fold.

♥ Pot odds is a system of comparing the potential profit of a bet to the possibility of winning a hand. When the profit is higher than the risk, the hand should be played.

♦ Big pots with a cheap price for entry are good values for drawing hands, and they're dangerous for big pairs.

♣ Raising is a powerful tool for manipulating pot odds and the size of the pot.

♠ Loose and passive players tend to lose money. Players generally become more profitable as they become tighter and more aggressive.

CHAPTER 6

Before the Flop

If all poker players were extreme versions of Moe, everyone would call your bets and nobody would raise. If they were all radical versions of Mickey, you could raise with trash under the gun and consistently **steal the blinds** because everyone (including the blinds) would fold thinking that you had **AA**.

In fact, most poker games have a mixture of players, and they're not always absolutely one way or another. So it is important that your poker strategy adjusts to accommodate the mood of the table. Your decisions should be in response to actions taken by specific opponents. A raise from Jay is entirely different than a raise from Mickey. And of course, your position (and theirs) plays an important role in your evaluation.

Opponents and Overall Strategy

In the previous chapter I described a "standard game" that has about six players. Now let's expand that definition.

Our standard game has one or two players who are solid or fairly good. One or two are **weak** (tend to play passively with little imagination), and one or two are live ones, very aggressive, wanting to gamble. Three or more players (usually more) stick around for the flop.

Now you might say, "Defining a standard game is all well and good, but what if I'm in a game with all good players? What should I do then?"

What you should do then is... Don't play!

"If they play long enough, they will lose."

—Sam "Ace" Rothstein (played by Robert De Niro), in *Casino*

There's an old poker proverb that says, "It doesn't do you much good to be rated the seventh-best player in the world if you're playing poker with the other six."

Realistically, you may find yourself in situations where you're outclassed. When that happens, just get out of the game if you can. If you can't leave (for political reasons), then just fold a lot. And speaking of folding...

More Fold 'Em than Hold 'Em

You can expect to see about thirty hands per hour at a full table (six opponents) if the dealers are reasonably competent. And of course, if every person at the table were to play every hand to its conclusion, then everyone would win on average about 1 in 6 hands, or about five hands per hour. Right?

But you're planning to fold some hands. Your opponents are surely expecting to fold some hands, too. If all of you fold about the same kind of hands, then you're still winning about five pots per hour, and your net profit is essentially zero.

To get an edge, you must do three things simultaneously: First, you've got to play tighter than the loose opponents, so your cards will beat theirs when they call you down. Second, you've got to be aggressive with the tight opponents, so they will release cards that might beat you. Third, you've got to build pots that you are likely to win, and spend little or nothing on hands that are losers.

So you won't be playing all of your hands, not even half of your hands. You'll be playing about 33 percent of them. And if 1 in 3 seems too low, then be thankful you're not playing at a full table in a casino (nine players), because the ideal action ratio in a casino is about 20 percent.

But here in our home game, you're going to be looser. People in private games expect some action. They'll play ridiculously bad hands in some situations, so you'll pick them off with good hands or maybe sometimes a mediocre hand that you would have folded against better players.

Calling or raising 1 in 3 hands means your average win ratio will be far lower than five pots per hour. This is mostly because you will inadvertently fold a few hands that would have been winners. Who woulda thunk that 8♦ 4♠ would turn into a straight flush? Nobody can predict that stuff. You could go broke chasing lightning and trying to put it into a bottle.

If you want to leave the table with a net win, then you must accept the fact that you'll voluntarily invest in about ten hands per hour, and you'll win maybe two or three pots per hour (about 30 percent of your action hands). And of course, there are streaks to consider. You might win five pots in a row, and then nothing for two hours. Seven or eight pots may be your entire profit for the evening. You don't want to make mistakes and lose those few hands. Similarly, you don't want those pots to be smaller because you misplayed the hands.

General Goals Before the Flop

Premium hands want few opponents, a large pot, and a high price for entry (thus discouraging bargain hands). Premium hands create this condition by raising to limit the field.

Bargain hands want to see the flop cheaply, so they limp in without a raise when possible. Conversely, if a bargain hand is in late position with a lot of callers, then it sometimes raises for value (doubles the size of the pot while getting excellent pot odds), or it might try to steal the blinds.

Average hands sometimes want few opponents and sometimes they want many opponents. It depends on the flop. That's why average hands (particularly the higher suited connectors) tend to play like premium hands in early position, and more like bargain hands in later position.

In the following pre-flop strategy, note that the term *raised pot* refers to action from a seat on your right. Raises from behind are covered in a later section.

And if I haven't made this clear already…This strategy is for *home games*. It's too loose and not aggressive enough for most casino play. On the other hand, if someone tries to play in your home game with a static (one-dimensional) casino-style approach, this strategy will help you suck the money from his wallet.

Early Position

EP Premium hands and an unraised pot: Raise with premium hands in early position about 75 percent of the time. Call about 25 percent of the time. These calls are strictly for deceptive purposes, so that people won't automatically assume that your early call (rather than a raise) is something less than a premium hand.

EP Premium hands and a raised pot: Reraise **AA**, **KK**, **QQ**, and **JJ**. You're trying to drive opponents out and isolate the raiser. Cap the pot with **AA**, **KK**, or **QQ** if possible, but evaluate your opponent and slow down with **JJ**; you may be up against a better pair. Similarly, you should just call with **AKn**. Reraise with **AKs** if a raise comes from behind and four or more players are in the hand, but with three or fewer just call any raise.

Keep in mind that **AKs** is a drawing hand; much of its value comes from the contributions of multiple opponents.

EP Average hands and an unraised pot: Raise 75 percent of the time with **AQ, AJ, KQs,** and call 25 percent of the time. Again, this is for deception. Always raise **TT** (because you really need to knock out opponents). Call with the rest of the average hands.

EP Average hands and a raised pot: Reraise **TT.** Call **AQs, AJs,** and **KQs.** Fold everything else *unless* the raiser is loose and tends to raise with less-than-premium hands. If he is loose, and if you reasonably expect many callers (four or more), then call with all the *suited* average hands, **AQn, KQn, 99,** and **88.** Toss the rest of the unsuited hands (**AJn, ATn, KJn, QJn,** and **JTn**).

EP Bargain hands and an unraised pot: Throw them all away unless the game is consistently loose/passive and you are certain to get many callers and no raises. If these perfect conditions exist, you can limp in. Remember, Mickey was in early position when he tried to limp in with low suited connectors, and he was buried by three raisers. So don't say I didn't warn you.

If the game is tight, and your opponents are experienced, you should occasionally raise with a bargain hand or something mediocre like **ATn** in early position just to throw the watchers off. But most of your opponents in home games won't be too observant. Don't waste your time or your chips unless someone is really studying your play.

EP Bargain hands and a raised pot: Throw them all away.

EP Two raises: If you're in the third seat and facing two raises, fold everything except premium hands. Follow the strategy for premium hands and a raised pot.

Premium hands	AA, KK, QQ, JJ, AK
Average hands	AQ, AJ, KQ, KJ, QJ, JT, AT, TT, 99, 88
Bargain hands	T9s and suited connectors down to 54s
	77 and pairs below
	Axs (suited hands containing an ace and any small card)
	KTs, QTs, J9s
Trash	Any hand that doesn't appear in the above three groups

Hands without an s or n indicate both suited and non-suited.

Note: This table is identical to the one in Chapter 4. It's repeated here so you don't have to flip back and forth between chapters.

Middle Position

MP Premium hands: Same strategy as in early position.

MP Average hands and an unraised pot: Raise TT, and call everything else.

MP Average hands and a raised pot: Same strategy as in early position.

MP Bargain hands: Same strategy as in early position.

MP Two raises or a capped pot: Play only premium hands (and TT if both raisers are loose and reckless). Follow premium strategy, with one exception. If it's three bets to you, don't cap the pot every time. Instead, just call about half the time and give the original raiser a chance to cap the pot. This will disguise your hand and give you information about the raiser. If she caps, then she probably has a premium hand. If she only calls, then she's probably holding a higher-quality average hand.

Late Position

LP Premium hands: Same strategy as in early and middle position.

LP Average hands and an unraised pot: Same strategy as in middle position unless you're first into the pot (no callers ahead). Then raise with everything about half the time. Call the other half.

LP Average hands and a raised pot: Same strategy as in early and middle position.

LP Bargain hands and an unraised pot: Fold all the bargain hands *except* pairs if there are three or fewer callers ahead of you. Stay in if there are four or more callers. If you're on the button with a lot of callers, occasionally raise with the bargain hands.

Conversely, if the game is tight and you're in late position with no callers, raise with a bargain hand in an attempt to steal the blinds.

LP Bargain hands and a raised pot: Fold everything unless nearly everyone is in the pot, the game is extremely loose, your opponents are weak, and you're on the button. Then call *carefully* with the bargain hands (see the tip on page 76).

LP Two raises or a capped pot: Same strategy as in middle position except if there are many callers (nearly the whole table). Then you can also play **AQs**, **AJs**, and **KQs**.

Tip

Calling a raise is safer when your action will end the round. This is not necessarily the same as being on the button. A late raiser to your right and active players to your left can trap you in a raising war.

The Blinds

Remember that the blinds are last to act before the flop and first to act in all the later rounds. Also keep in mind that the big blind has already bet, so the only decision here is to raise or call a raise.

Generally, you should play the blinds with a late-position strategy, but occasionally you can play a bit looser if there was an early raiser and a lot of callers, because you might be looking at a huge pile o' chips and a single extra bet as the price for entry. Pot odds might be 10:1 or better. If that's the case, go ahead and call a raise with all the average hands, bargain hands, and even some marginal trash like Kxs and T8s.

If you have a bargain hand or marginal trash (Qxs, Txs, 89n, Axn, and similar combinations) in the little blind with a lot of callers and no raises, call for half a bet or less. Fold if there has been a raise.

The issue of defending the blind against a possible steal is a complex subset of poker strategy. You won't have to face this much in loose games because opportunities to steal are rare. If there are other callers, simply fold when your hand doesn't warrant a call. If you're heads-up against a late raiser, fold the first time it happens and raise the second time (with a bargain hand or better).

A Raise From Behind

If you play a starting hand correctly, then it's always worth a call and possibly a reraise when a raise comes from behind. Pot odds will help you make this decision.

What if you incorrectly play a hand and find yourself trapped holding a bargain combination while facing two or three opponents and a raise? Just fold. Learn from the mistake and don't do that again. Recognize that the table is more aggressive than you thought. You'll need to tighten up. Jettison the bargain hands in middle position. Jettison the unsuited average hands.

Exceptions, Exceptions

The more you learn about hold 'em, the more you'll find exceptions to the pre-flop strategy I have outlined. There are situations when it is correct to raise with trash, and there are times when a premium hand clearly does not merit a raise.

There are plenty of experts who would *not* raise TT in early position, and some who *would* raise 99. Other disputed hands include AT, A9, JT, and 88. In fact, every hand has its exceptions.

The lesson here is that you shouldn't play like an automaton. Instead, you should consider position, the pot, and your opponents, then choose the best strategy for that particular situation. In most cases you'll find the best strategy is the one outlined on the previous pages.

If you come across a situation that has you completely stumped, follow this advice: when in doubt, throw it out.

Essentially

♠ Only about 33 percent of hold 'em starting hands are playable in a private game, and about one-third of those go on to become winners. So it's important to identify strong hands quickly and play them for maximum profit.

♥ Many hands are unplayable in early position. The range of hands that are playable increases when a seat is closer to the button.

♦ Premium hands want few opponents and a large pot. Bargain hands want to see the flop cheaply, so they limp in without a raise when possible. Average hands tend to play like premium hands in early position, and more like bargain hands in late position.

♣ When in doubt, throw it out.

CHAPTER 7

The Flop and Beyond

The flop is the pivotal moment in hold 'em. Five of the seven cards (71 percent) have been revealed. The character of the hand is generally set, and three rounds of betting are ahead. The flop is the best time to drop an obvious loser or begin the process of pumping a hopeful winner. It's also the time when you must realistically anticipate the various ways a hand might develop.

For example, let's go back to a scenario from Chapter 5; you have QJ in late position and a rainbow flop of **984**. What happens if the turn produces a queen? That might look good to you, but it would look even better to someone holding JT. And what if the pot was raised before the flop? The pre-flop raiser might have a hand that would beat you either way: AA, KK, QQ, or AQ.

So pot odds may suggest a call on the flop, but the implied odds may indicate a fold.

The Big Shift

Recently I sat down in a poker game that had just started, and I was fortunate enough to play my first hand on the button. The dealer gave me two red aces. I was intending to raise, but the betting was capped before action reached me. Everyone was in for four bets. Yikes! So I called.

The flop was **9♣ 8♣ 7♣**. There was a bet and three calls ahead of me. What were my chances of winning this pot?

Not very good. Someone could have made a straight or a flush on the flop. And if not, then someone was surely drawing to one or both. Beyond that, my biggest concern was that **A♣** might be out there waiting for another club. That ace in someone else's hand lowered the probability (already slim) that my hand could improve.

THE FACT IS...

The button (dealer) position in a new flop game is determined by a draw of cards. Each player draws a card from a shuffled deck, and the high card gets the button.

A fold here was correct. But I hesitated. The pot was gargantuan because of the betting on the previous round, and the cost here was only one bet with me on the button. The pot odds were 40:1. It would be a cheap gamble. Maybe lightning would strike and an ace would fall. Then maybe the board would pair to give me a full house. Yada yada...

I threw my hand away. No gambling for me.

The turn was a blank (a meaningless card, a **2♠**). Again, there was a bet and three calls. Keep in mind that a call here on the turn cost twice as much as the previous round. The river was **K♣**. There was one bet and three calls. **A♣ K♥** took the pot (with an ace-high club flush). The other hands were **Q♣ J♣**, **K♠ K♦**, and **9♦ 9♥**.

The lesson here is that a premium hand quickly can become nearly worthless on the flop. But some people become so enamored with their big pocket pair or their suited high cards that they cannot shift gears when the hand is hopelessly dead or severely damaged. They just keep betting, raising, or calling until the bitter end.

So once the flop comes, you should forget about how wonderful your hand was two seconds ago. Now you're looking at a new hand, and you'll find that it generally fits into one of the following categories.

Strong hand: A combination that is the nuts or unlikely to be beaten.

Vulnerable leading hand: A hand that is definitely leading, but could easily become a second-best hand in a later round. Trips is a typical example of a vulnerable leading hand.

Weak leading hand: This hand is probably leading but extremely vulnerable. There are a lot of ways it could lose. An example would be **AQ** with a flop of **QJ8**. If **AQ** was the only pre-flop raiser, then it's probably top pair (though it's entirely possible that someone else is holding **QJ** for two pairs, or **T9** for a straight). Either way, **AQ** is vulnerable to anyone holding a nine or ten, especially **JT**, **AT**, **J9**, **QT**, and **Q9**. There might even be an **88** lurking out there.

Second-best hand: Using the previous example, someone holding **AJ** would be second best to **AQ**. **AQ** would be second best to **QJ**. Players who are second best and don't realize it are the primary source of profit in poker. My red aces are another example of a second-best hand (actually it was third best on the flop).

Drawing hand: This is typically a four-card flush or four-card straight looking for a fifth card, but it also includes any hand that is clearly an underdog and hoping to improve. One example would be two pairs drawing to a full house when the board and pattern of betting indicate that someone has a flush.

Obvious loser: A hand like **8♦ 7♦** against a board like **Q♥ Q♠ J♥** with a raise and reraise ahead is an obvious loser. Hands competing with the nuts or in other unwinnable situations are said to be **drawing dead**

General Goals on the Flop and Afterwards

Strong hands want to extract the maximum amount of money from the table. It's a pleasant job, but not as easy as you might imagine because experienced opponents can often tell when someone is holding a better combination, and they drop.

Drawing hands generally want to continue as cheaply as possible, though they sometimes want to build the pot if the pot odds will exceed the probability of hitting their hand.

Tip

The value of a starting hand often shifts dramatically on the flop. A hand that seemed anemic may be suddenly strong, and a strong starter such as **AKs** may become almost worthless. A sudden shift doesn't necessarily mean that a pre-flop raise was incorrect, but the flop does create a new situation that you should recognize.

Vulnerable and weak leading hands want to make each round as *expensive* as possible so that drawing hands won't stick around and improve.

Obvious losers want to quickly identify their unhappy condition and stop putting money in the pot.

Second-best hands are somewhere between obvious losers and drawing hands. They can improve and win, but they often don't, so they want to see the turn and river very cheaply or for free, otherwise they're looking to fold.

Reading the Flop

Position plays an important role on the flop (as it does in every round of hold 'em). A bet, raise, and reraise tells you a lot, as does a bet and long line of callers. It also helps to remember how an opponent played pre-flop. Here are a few examples:

This is a flop that looks good to **AA**, **KK**, and **QQ** (assuming they're not all simultaneously competing). Of course, this is a strong flop for **JJ**, and it also looks inviting to **AJ**, **KJ**, **QJ**, and **JT**. See how the latter hands can be crushed by the former? All of them are vulnerable to **T9** and **65**. How can you tell who has what? Let's say that you're holding **AJ** and you were the only raiser before the flop. It's likely that your pair of jacks with an ace kicker is the best hand. But if you called a pre-flop raise, **AJ** is possibly second best (behind a higher pocket pair). This is nearly certain if the same player raises again.

This is the kind of flop that usually gets a lot of action and breaks a lot of bankrolls. **KK** is probably the best hand here if there was a lot of pre-flop raising. If there wasn't, then someone may have limped in with **AT** or **T9**. Any of these three hands will hurt **AA**, **QQ**, **JJ**, **AK**, **AQ**, **AJ**, **KQ**, **QJ**, or **KJ** unless a ten falls and makes a straight for anyone holding an ace. Another diamond may finish a flush. If the board pairs then the straight or flush may be beaten by a full house. One way or another it's going to be a monster pot with a wild finish.

This flop turns **AKn** into semi-trash. It's also bad news for **AJn**, **KJn**, **JJ**, and **TT**. Anyone holding a queen is in good shape unless another spade falls to make a flush, or another low card appears to fill in a straight.

Flops like this usually produce small pots because hands without an ace are unlikely to stick around if anyone bets. **AK** is a strong favorite over other hands that have an ace and a lower kicker. **A7** has a full house but may still be beaten by a higher full house if the wrong card comes on the turn or the river. It happens.

This is a scary flop for **A♦ A♥**. There are a lot of ways to lose, including to a straight, a flush on the turn or river, or two pairs. Note that high cards next to each other in rank or one-gapped often give opponents two pairs.

THE FACT IS...

The probability of your **AK** flopping a pair or better is about 35 percent, or 1 in 3.

This is the kind of flop you'll love when holding **88**, **99**, or **TT** (as well as higher pairs). It's death to big unpaired cards.

There are countless more examples, but these few flops give you a taste of the thought process and the dynamics of hold 'em at this stage. The best way to handle these situations is largely determined by your position and the actions of your opponents.

Bet or Check, Raise or Fold

Strategy on the flop and afterwards is much more complex and situational than pre-flop strategy. That's because there are only 1,326 possible two-card starting hands but more than 2.5 million five-card combinations. Nevertheless, hands of a certain type generally can be played similarly.

Two Overcards

If you've got no pair but two strong overcards with a non-threatening board (example: **AK** with a flop of **T62** rainbow), it's often a good idea to come out betting if nobody has yet entered the pot. Everyone may fold to you. If not, then you'll at least thin the field. A raise from behind will alert you to the fact that somebody has a pair or better. In most cases you should fold if someone raises your overcards. But don't do it automatically. Consider the size of the pot, the flop, and your opponent.

Tip

Middle or bottom pair is significantly weaker than top pair, and it's often unplayable unless you have a strong kicker and the opposition is clearly weak. Example: You hold **AT** and the flop is **JT6**. You bet in early position and get only two callers. It's probable that you're up against a ten with a lower kicker or opponents drawing to straights.

If someone bets ahead of you, evaluate the flop, and then fold if the pot is not large enough. Beware of a board that has suited cards, straight cards, high connectors, or high pairs. Yes, it's tough to part with **AK** and other big connectors, but calling with no draw and an ace-high is often a waste of money.

Top Pair, Two Pairs, and Trips

If you've got top pair with a strong kicker, two pairs, or trips, then come out betting on the flop. Raise if someone bets ahead of you. Opponents calling behind you rather than raising would generally indicate that you're probably the best hand (unless you're up against a monster combination that is waiting for the next round).

Straight or Better

Flopping a nut-straight, nut-flush, or better isn't too common. Hands like these should be slow-played on the flop. Checking and calling will lure people into hanging around for the turn and double bets. That's when you should become aggressive. On the other hand, don't slow-play without the nuts. Be especially careful with low cards (example: **87** with **JT9**).

Obvious Losers

Check and fold if the flop misses you completely and you don't have two overcards. Fold if you've got middle or bottom pair with a weak kicker (example: **98** and **AQ9**). Fold if you have top pair with a weak kicker, and you're facing a raise (example: **A5** and **AQJ**). Fold when you're clearly second best unless you have a good draw to the best hand and favorable pot odds. Generally, if a hand is not worth a bet or raise, then it's not worth a call (except when drawing to the nuts or near-nuts).

Drawing Hands

Are you drawing to a strong hand? If yes, then bet in early position unless you fear a raise. If a pre-flop raiser is behind you, it may be best to check and call. Or you might even check-raise if there is a bet behind you and then a lot of callers (thus dramatically pumping up your pot odds).

If you're drawing to a strong hand *and* you've got top pair, just play it aggressively. But what if someone raises you?

A Short Course in Poker ESP

You've been raised on the flop. What is the opponent raising with? Think back to the way he played his hand before the flop. You can usually put an opponent on a hand (accurately read what he's holding) by matching the board to pre-flop and post-flop betting. Here's an example.

Let's say you hold K♦ J♦ in late position. There were four callers before you. You call, and the button folds. The flop comes:

Everyone checks to you. You bet, and the player in seat one raises (a check-raise). Everyone behind him folds to you. What is the raiser holding?

It's unlikely that he's holding K6 or Q6 unless he's someone who calls pre-flop in early position with complete trash. Also, he didn't raise before the flop, so it's not likely that he's holding AA, AK, KK, or QQ (unless he was trying to be deceptive before the flop by not raising).

On the other hand, he check-raised on the flop. This indicates strength, though not overwhelming strength. If the hand is very strong (such as KK, making trips), seat one may have been more likely to slow-play (call rather than raise, to feign weakness and thus keep KJ in the hand).

Would seat one check-raise middle pair (a hand like AQ or QJ)? Probably not, unless he is *very sure* that it would knock his opponent out. Would he check-raise a straight draw? Maybe. This would be a semi-bluff. We'll talk more about semi-bluffs later.

Would he check-raise top pair or better. Yes, that's more likely. Maybe he has 66 in the pocket, giving him low trips. If not trips, then probably a king and...What is the second card? Could it be a KQ? Yes, it could.

Should you call? Probably not. The only legitimate hands you can beat at this point are KT and K9.

In the real-life hand, I was the person in seat one who check-raised, and KJ called my check-raise on the flop. The next card was another queen, so the board was K♥ Q♦ 6♠ Q♥.

Tip

I checked the turn, KJ bet, and I raised him again. Two check-raises in a row. If you were KJ, would you release now?

KJ called. The river was 7♠. I bet, and KJ called. I turned up K♠ Q♣ to make queens full of kings. KJ flipped up his hand (a pair of kings) and said, "I didn't think you had it."

He thought I was bluffing, so he called to keep me honest.

The Other Side of the Looking Glass

Now let's look at the hand we just reviewed from my perspective. I was holding K♠ Q♣ against a fairly loose and aggressive table. A pre-flop raise would not have knocked out many players, so I called under the gun rather than raising.

When two pairs flopped I was pleased but wary, because a hand like this can go bad in a lot of different ways.

First, there is the possibility of a backdoor flush (two suited cards falling on the turn and river). If those cards were diamonds, that would have given K♦ J♦ a flush. A "runner-runner" to fill in a backdoor flush happens about 4 percent of the time.

Second, I feared a straight draw. Anyone holding JT had eight outs (a 32 percent chance of beating my two pairs). Anyone holding AJ or AT had four outs. And of course, KJ could win with a backdoor straight. Also, I was concerned about the possibility that KK or QQ had limped in, or maybe 66.

So I wanted to drive out drawing hands, nuke their pot odds, and unmask stronger hands by getting them to play back at me (if there were stronger hands out there).

I also knew that the guy in seat five was very aggressive, and I figured he would bet if nobody else came in before him. So I checked, and sure enough, seat five bet. Then I raised. Everyone folded to him (exactly as I wanted). Seat five gave me a disgusted look, and called.

When the queen came on the turn (giving me a full house), I checked immediately, as if I hadn't looked at the card. The impression I was trying to give was that I was planning to check, hoping perhaps for a "free card" (see the next section for more on free cards). I expected him to take this as a sign of weakness, and he did. He bet, and I raised him. Now he was angry. When a blank hit on the river, I bet. I was sure he would call just to see my cards. And I was right!

Raising to Get a Free Card

A free card is a powerful multilayered strategy that is generally unknown among casual poker players. Here's how it works.

You're in late position. Four people call ahead of you before the flop and you call with A♦ T♦. The big blind checks. The flop delivers:

Four players check and the fifth bets. What should you do?

Well, it depends a lot on the people in your game, but a raise here might be a good tactic. Here's the reasoning. You may have the best hand right now, but even if you don't, a raise will make you look as if you do. And you have a 1 in 3 chance of making the nut flush.

If the turn fails to help anyone, your opponents may check to you because they'll want to avoid another raise.

They'll expect you to bet, but you won't bet. You'll check and end the round. They'll be relieved, but it's you who has reason to celebrate. You've just given yourself a free card. It's an extra opportunity to improve your hand without investing anything in the process.

THE FACT IS...

A "free card" is actually a cheap card. You bet or raise on an early round as a semi-bluff, with the hope that everyone will check to you in a later round. If your hand doesn't improve by the later round, then you check and take a "free" card.

Conversely, you don't want to give away free cards. Generally, you should bet the flop *and* the turn when your hand is leading. Make opponents pay to see the cards.

By the way, betting or raising a hand that is currently not best, but could become best, is known as a semi-bluff. You're hoping to win the pot right there, but if someone calls then there's a chance your hand will improve.

An even better example of a semi-bluff would be limping in with A♠ 6♠ in early position. The flop comes 9♠ 6♥ 2♦. You have the potential for making a backdoor flush, and five outs to two pairs or trips. What would your opponents have? Remember that nobody raised before the flop. A bet here might take the pot.

The Turn and the River

The noose tightens on the turn. Bets double, and the probability of improving drops dramatically. By this point you should be leading, or bluffing well, or you should have a clear idea of how you will win if someone calls you on the end. If you don't have a plan, then check or get out of the hand. Remember that bankrolls are mostly consumed by too much calling on the flop and turn, not by bad beats on the river.

If you've got the best hand, then bet it. Or go for a check-raise if you're reasonably certain that someone will bet behind you. But watch out. An opponent may have semi-bluffed on the flop, so if you try a check-raise, you may inadvertently give away a free card on the turn.

Betting or Calling on the End

Folding on the end is rarely correct unless you're reasonably certain that a hand is a loser. Pot odds are usually so enormous by this point that any realistic chance for a win deserves a call. That's why Erin called on the end in the Chapter 2 example. Of course, if a hand is clearly busted, you should save yourself the bet.

Conversely, it's rarely correct to bet on the end unless the bet is a pure bluff, or your hand is exceptionally strong. That's because (as I explained in the previous paragraph) good players will call you only if they might win. That's not a problem when you're holding the nuts or something close, but it's a big problem when the lead is not so well defined. You might be holding a big pair of aces and find yourself beaten by two pairs. Checking in this situation would save money (that's what Erin did, and she saved herself the cost of a reraise). Remember, betting on the end is pointless if only the losers fold.

Tip

Even bad players get good hands from time to time. Opponents who raise on the turn are rarely bluffing. Those who bet or raise on the river are (almost) never bluffing.

Bluffing

You may have noticed that I barely used the word *bluff* in this book. That's because good players don't bluff a lot. Instead they semi-bluff, raise for value, and make other strategic bets that confuse their opponents.

Pure deception is like pepper. You should use it sparingly. The complexity of your basic game should be the major source of misdirection. Besides, everyone has seen poker in the movies, or they watch the World Poker Tour, and they imagine themselves capable of exposing a bluff.

Also remember that it's nearly impossible to bluff multiple opponents. Somebody is going to have a hand that is worth a call.

Exceptions, Exceptions

Sometimes you can read the table perfectly and win with middle or bottom pair. Sometimes you can miss the flop completely and finish with trips on the river. Sometimes it is correct to chase with a second-best hand. Poker has millions of "sometimes" situations. As I mentioned in Chapter 6, you should not play like an automaton, but the strategies here are optimal in the majority of circumstances.

Essentially

♠ The flop is the pivotal moment in hold 'em. Five of the seven cards (71 percent) have been revealed. Hands at this stage generally fall into four categories: strong leading hands, vulnerable leading hands, drawing hands, and losers.

♥ An opponent's actions before the flop and on the flop can often give you a good idea of what he's holding.

♦ Generally, very strong hands should be slow-played until the turn. Vulnerable hands should be aggressively played. Drawing hands should be played in ways that maximize their value when they hit. Losers should be dropped.

♣ Never give a free card when your hand is leading and vulnerable. Take a free card whenever possible if your hand is second best and hoping to improve.

♠ Calling on the end is usually correct unless your hand is an obvious loser.

♥ Checking on the end is best when your hand is leading but vulnerable.

♦ Bluffing is a tactic that should be used sparingly. The complexity of your basic game should be the major source of misdirection.

PART THREE

Seven-Card Stud and Other Games

CHAPTER 8

Seven-Card Stud

New poker versions are easy to learn when you understand poker basics such as pot odds, the power of folding, the importance of selecting the best starting hands, and other fundamental concepts we covered in the previous chapters.

Of course, specific strategies change with each version (sometimes dramatically), but keep in mind that the underlying systems remain the same. A raise is a tool for getting opponents to drop. Vulnerable hands should be protected. Drawing hands should be played cheaply, and so forth.

In this chapter and the next we cover the most popular poker versions after hold 'em. We begin here with seven-card stud.

Rules of the Game

Seven-card stud doesn't use community cards, as hold 'em does. Instead, each player builds a poker hand from seven personal cards, four of which are exposed.

The game begins with an ante from all the players. The amount of the ante is usually a fraction of a full bet. For example, an ante of fifty cents or one dollar would be typical for a 3-6 or 4-8 game. A five-dollar ante would be about right for a 30-60 game.

Each player receives two cards face down and then one card face up. This first exposed card is called the door card

Tip

Suit is used to determine the bring-in when cards are of the same rank. The suits are valued lowest to highest in alphabetical order: clubs, diamonds, hearts, spades.

The player with the *lowest door card* is required to make a small initial bet, called a bring-in. In a 3-6 or 4-8 game this might be one or two dollars (something less than the game minimum). The bring-in can also make a full bet if she chooses.

The player to the left of the bring-in can call the bring-in, raise to the game minimum, raise a full bet if the bring-in was a full bet, or fold. Action proceeds clockwise from that position. This round is called third street (for obvious reasons). Subsequent rounds are also named for the number of cards in a hand, though seventh street is sometimes called the river.

Action on fourth street and later rounds begins with the player who has the *highest exposed hand* rather than the lowest card. If two high hands are equal, then the high hand to the dealer's left acts first.

Fourth through sixth streets are dealt face up and seventh street is dealt face down. Bets double on fifth street.

The Importance of Live Cards

Much of the strategy of seven-card stud involves the concept of live cards. Let's say you're dealt a starting hand of:

The jack of hearts is the door card (exposed card). Looks good, right? But you look out on the table and see in other hands a jack, a ten, a queen, an ace, and two low cards that are diamonds. That means the probability of your hand improving has dropped dramatically. Two of your outs for trips or a full house are gone. And some of your straight and flush cards are dead too. That doesn't mean necessarily that the hand is unplayable, but you need to handle it carefully. If you get a lot of action from the ace, then you may be up against a bigger pair, with only a few ways to improve.

So you must evaluate other hands and calculate how they affect yours. Also, you need to remember cards that were folded by your opponents.

Let's say you have:

And your opponent is showing:

If you saw A♠ go into the muck, then you know absolutely that your opponent doesn't have three aces in his hand. Does he have two pairs aces and eights, or aces and sixes? How about a full house eights full of aces, or sixes full of aces? You've got to think back to the cards you saw exposed as the hand progressed.

Starting Hands

As you might expect, suited cards, pairs, trips, and connectors make the most powerful starting hands. While I don't want to imply any *exact* parallels with hold 'em starting hands, it's fair to say that the same general patterns apply. You should play big pairs hard and fast. Drawing hands should be played cheaply or raised for value when a lot of people are in the pot.

Trips should be slow-played on third street, and then raised on fourth or fifth street depending on how many

Tip

Beware of a paired door card in an opponent's hand. This dramatically increases the probability that you're up against trips (or better), particularly when the door card is of a higher rank.

players are still in the hand and the degree of strength they're showing. If you don't have any of the above and no big cards, then fold the hand.

Later Streets

Five of the seven cards (71 percent of the hand) have been revealed by fifth street. This is where bets double, so it's best to fold here if you're not leading and you don't have a strong draw. Remember that the overall probability of seeing any particular seven-card combination is *exactly the same* in seven-card stud as in hold 'em, but the extra variable is live cards. So use the charts from Chapter 5 and subtract outs when you see them in other hands.

Pot Odds in Seven-Card Stud

There's a popular saying among seven-card stud players: If you call a bet on fifth street, then you've bought yourself a ticket to seventh street. What that means is that it's rarely correct to fold *after* fifth street unless you're absolutely sure that you're beaten and drawing dead. The reason for this is that the pots (and the corresponding pot odds) get very big by the time you reach sixth and seventh street. That extra round of betting in seven-card stud, compared to flop games, really adds up.

But this doesn't mean you should play every hand in seven-card stud to its conclusion. Rather, you need to be extremely selective on third and fourth street, more selective than you might otherwise be when playing a flop game.

For example, it's easy and relatively cheap to limp in with a small pair when you're playing hold 'em. If that pair turns into trips on the flop, then you've got a good shot of winning the pot.

But in seven-card stud, there are two betting rounds before you see five cards, so a small pair isn't such a good value. Thus a hand such as 8♦ 4♠ 4♣ is rarely worth playing. But 4♠ 4♣ "in the hole" with A♣ as a door card might be worth a call, or even a semi-bluff raise if you feel that you have good control of the table.

But once again, it all depends on what the rest of the table is showing.

Essentially

♠ There are no community cards in seven-card stud. A player receives seven personal cards. The first two are dealt face down, then four face up, and the last one face down.

♥ Action on the first round begins with the lowest exposed card. Action on later rounds begins with the highest exposed hand.

♦ Much of the strategy in seven-card stud involves live cards. The potential strength of your hand is affected by cards you see in other hands.

♣ Suited cards, high pairs, trips, and connectors make the most powerful starting hands in seven-card stud.

♠ You should fold early if your hand is mediocre. It's rarely correct to fold after fifth street unless you're absolutely sure that you're beaten and drawing dead.

CHAPTER 9

Other Poker Versions

There are dozens of poker versions besides hold 'em and seven-card stud. Most fall into one of three categories. Flop games are variations of hold 'em, stud games are variations of seven-card stud, and draw games are variations of five-card draw. Since we haven't covered five-card draw yet, we'll begin with that game.

Some people think (incorrectly) that five-card draw is the "original" poker contest. Indeed, it was the most popular poker version in the Old West. Let's say you were in a crowded saloon and you heard the steely voice of Wyatt Earp or Wild Bill Hickok snarling, "Draw, you scoundrel!" It is likely the conversation was about a poker hand rather than a gun. And of course, poor Mr. Hickok lost his life while playing five-card draw. He was holding aces and eights when he was shot in the back. The famous gunslinger's last words were, "The old duffer...He broke me on the hand."

So five-card draw is definitely very old, but there are even older poker versions, including five-card no draw and five-card stud, so draw isn't as "original" and "pure" as some people might suppose. And yet, it is the poker version you probably played with your grandpa when you were five, and everyone remembers it from the movies. It's an old favorite. Here is how it goes:

Five-Card Draw

The game uses an ante, and a standard rotating dealer. Five cards are dealt face down to each player. Action begins to the left of the dealer.

In the "classic" version you need jacks or better to open. If nobody has jacks or better, then the cards are mucked, another round of antes is added to the pot, and a new hand is dealt.

If someone opens with a bet, then action proceeds in typical poker fashion. After everyone is finished calling, raising, or folding, players who are still in the pot have an opportunity to **draw**. Players can surrender one or more of their cards and receive replacements from the dealer. Or a player can stand pat.

A second round of betting comes after the draw. Action begins with the opener from the previous round. After the betting, everyone in the pot reveals his or her cards for the showdown.

Strategy for Five-Card Draw

You've heard it since you were a child...Don't draw to an inside straight.

Also remember that the number of cards you draw says something about your hand. Drawing three cards is equivalent to screaming, "I have a high pair!" Drawing two cards indicates trips, or a pair with a kicker. Drawing one card tells someone that you're trying to fill in a straight or a flush, or you're trying to improve two pairs. Unless, of course, you're bluffing.

By the way, there is a mathematically optimized draw strategy for draw poker. It's mostly used by professional gamblers for games such as video poker, but the strategy (for improving your hand) works equally well for the live version of the game. In brief, it is a hierarchy of hand values. Obviously, at the top of the list is a pair of jacks...or better. You hold the cards of value and discard the rest.

 **Tip**

If you don't have jacks or better, then hold a four-card flush (and draw one card). If you don't have a four-card flush, then hold a four-card "outside" straight, then low pairs, then big cards, in that order of importance.

The full draw strategy (which requires a chapter of its own) can be found in *The Smarter Bet™ Guide to Slots and Video Poker* (Sterling Publishing).

And of course, action and pot odds will tell you if a particular drawing hand is viable. In many cases, you should just fold rather than call and draw.

Lowball

Lowball is five-card draw played for low. In other words, the lowest (worst) hand wins rather than the highest. Straights and flushes don't count in lowball, so the worst (best) hand is **A-2-3-4-5**. This is called a wheel or bicycle. The next-best hand is **A-2-3-4-6**, third best is **A-2-3-5-6**, and so on. A hand such as **2-3-4-5-8** is much worse, and anything above ten is generally unplayable.

If you're a beginner, it's easy to get confused about what beats what when playing lowball. The solution is to determine the highest hand as you would normally, then flip the decision. Thus **2-4-5-7-8** would lose to **2-3-5-7-9** when playing for high, but it would win when playing for low because nine is higher than eight.

Omaha Hi/Lo

The original version of this game is called Omaha. It's hold 'em played with *four cards* in the pocket, and *exactly two* of those four cards must be used to make a hand. So if you have:

And the board shows:

You don't have a straight or a flush. You have a pair of aces. The best five-card Omaha hand from the above seven cards is **A♣ A♦ K♣ 9♣ 7♥** (using two of the four cards in your hand).

These days Omaha is usually played as Omaha hi/lo. The high hand splits the pot with the lowest hand that is eight or better (which really means eight-high or worse). The low hand in the previous example is **A♦ 3♥ 4♥ 5♣ 6♣**.

If there is no qualifying low hand (eight or better), then high hand takes the whole pot.

Omaha Hi/Lo Starting Hands

Omaha hi/lo is a wild contest because so many cards are in play and there are so many ways to win. Pots often become very large because everyone figures they have a shot. A lone pair of jacks or queens can often win an entire pot in hold 'em, but this rarely happens in Omaha hi/lo. If an ace and king hit the board, it's nearly certain that someone is holding at least one of those cards, maybe both. High pairs and even two pairs are anemic hands. A typical winner is a straight or better. And remember, half the pot goes to a low hand. Ideally, you want to scoop the pot, by winning both high and low.

The best starting hands are combinations that can work for both high and low. Examples would be A♠ A♦ 2♦ 3♠, A♥ K♦ 3♦ 4♥, or A♣ 2♣ K♥ K♦.

A playable but less flexible hand would be A♠ K♠ Q♥ Q♣, because this could only capture high. Examples of hands to toss include Q♦ J♥ 8♠ 9♠ and K♦ J♠ T♥ 9♦.

Note that these hands could be played as two-card combinations in hold 'em, but they rarely hold up in Omaha hi/lo.

Other Games

Pineapple is hold 'em played with three pocket cards. One of the three cards must be discarded on the flop. The rest of the game plays like hold 'em.

Razz is seven-card stud played for low. The way to win at razz is to start with three low cards (A-2-3 is best), and keep track of how many lows are still alive as the hand develops. Seven-card stud can also be played hi/lo.

Five-card stud is similar to seven-card stud, but each player begins with one card face down and one card face up. There is a round of betting and then one additional card is dealt face up to each player. Another round of betting follows, another card is dealt face up, and so forth. The showdown comes after everyone has five cards.

Southern cross (or **iron cross**) is a classic home-style poker game in which five community cards are dealt face down in the form of a cross (three across, one high, one low). Each player gets five personal cards, face down. Then the five community cards are revealed one-by-one, outside cards first, and the middle card is revealed last. A round of betting occurs as each card is revealed. A player must use two cards from his hand and three in a row from the cross to make a five-card poker hand.

Anaconda (or **pass the trash**) is another classic home-style poker version. Everyone gets seven cards, face down. There is a round of betting, and then each player passes three cards to his left. Another round of betting, and two cards are passed to the left. One more round, and one card is passed. Then each player chooses five of seven cards (discards the other two) and rolls the five-card hand one card at a time… of course with a round of betting after each card is revealed.

Tip

If you want a strip poker game to last a while, limit the number of raises to one or two per round (rather than the traditional three or four). On the other hand, if you want to speed things up, raise the antes.

Strip Poker

Strip poker isn't really a poker version. Rather, it's a method of betting. Nevertheless, it's the ultimate poker home game. The object of the contest is to get your opponents naked.

You can play it with any version of poker, but some versions are more "expensive" than others. How quickly do you want the game to come to a conclusion?

Obviously, a contest such as hold 'em will last longer than a game with a bazillion betting rounds such as pass the trash.

Five-card draw is probably the slowest (and most tantalizing) version for strip poker.

Losing Your Shirt

Clothing is the coin of the realm in strip poker. Each item of clothing counts as one unit of value. So a pair of shoes is two items, a bra is one, socks are two, and pantyhose is one. Jewelry, hair bands, glasses, and the like don't count unless you want to make the contest last longer.

If you bend the rules to include non-clothing items, then beware of people who bend the rules further to keep their clothes on. I know one guy who played a heads-up game with a magazine-model friend of his in West Hollywood. At the end of two hours he had beat her for forty-seven bets and she was still fully clothed. He had no idea a girl could have so many combs, clips, toe rings, earrings, and such on her body.

Assuming everyone is playing fair, the general rule is that outside clothes come off first. And when a piece of clothing comes off, it stays off, regardless of who wins the pot. In other words, clothing that has been wagered once can be used for betting thereafter, but not for wearing.

In a game with three or more players, if a player loses everything (and is thus naked), that player traditionally stays naked until the rest of the players complete the game. Strip poker is like a poker tournament, the contest continues until one person wins it all.

In practice, you'll find that the speed at which the game concludes is often a result of who is eliminated first. If the first two contestants out are...um...bent on attracting attention to themselves, this may cause the game to break up quickly. Also, let's say you have the hots for someone (Samantha, Sammy, Sam, whatever), and that person busts out early. Would you rather win the tournament, or quickly lose everything yourself, and thus be free to offer (or request) a consoling back rub?

As with all poker contests, a lot of what happens in strip poker depends on the personalities and attitudes of the contestants.

Terms of Endearment

Strip poker is obviously the kind of game where a phrase such as "flop a monster" or "jam the pot" can have a double meaning. So be cautious when using standard poker vocabulary.

For example, avoid saying, "Can you beat my nut flush?" Someone may take you literally. Likewise, it's wise to refrain from exclamations as, "Please, dealer, fill in my backdoor straight!" Unless of course...well...we won't get into that.

Essentially

♠ Five-card draw uses an ante, and a rotating dealer. Five cards are dealt face down to each player. There is a round of betting, a draw (players can replace cards), another round of betting, and a showdown.

♥ In the "classic" version of five-card draw, you need jacks or better to open. If nobody has jacks or better, then the cards are mucked, new antes are added to the pot, and a new hand is dealt.

♦ Omaha is similar to hold 'em except it is played with four cards in the pocket. Exactly two of those cards must be used to make a poker hand. In the hi/lo version of Omaha, the pot is split between the player holding the high hand and the player holding the low hand (when the low hand is eight or "better").

♣ Other poker versions include lowball (five-card draw played for low), razz (seven-card stud played for low), pineapple, southern cross, and anaconda. There are dozens of poker variations.

♠ The object of strip poker is to get your opponents naked. Each item of clothing counts as one unit of value. Jewelry, hair bands, glasses, and the like don't count unless you want to make the contest last longer (and you want to drive yourself crazy with frustration).

PART FOUR

Practical Issues

CHAPTER 10

Hosting a Poker Game

Okay, so you want to organize a poker game... Why? Is it strictly about winning, or is there another reason for the gathering? Do you want to bond with your pals? Do you crave sandwiches, beer, and cards at midnight? Is the game your weekly "night out" away from the spouse? Is it an opportunity to score political points by hosting your boss and his cronies? Is it a way to get laid? Is it just about being with interesting people?

There are many reasons for organizing a home game, so it pays to clearly understand yourself (and your motives). Basic issues such as the stakes, the opponents, and even the starting time and length of the game, are best determined by examining your larger goals.

And speaking of larger goals... Back in Chapter 1 I told you that the goal in poker is to win the most money. I wrote, "Every element of the game, every decision you make, every moment at the table is entirely about this one purpose. Never let yourself be distracted by any other poker goals."

This is how you win when playing poker. But of course, there is a larger game of life that you're playing simultaneously. Your poker game is just one hand in that bigger contest. And by now you surely know, winning one hand is less important than winning the bigger game.

Let's say Uncle Charlie is a bad poker player. Do you want him sitting in your game and losing his money?

> *"Money won is twice as sweet as money earned."*
>
> —Eddie Felson (played by Paul Newman), in *The Color of Money*

The answer might be yes if he's filthy rich (especially if you're not in his will). On the other hand, Charlie might be living on a fixed income, and your spouse might be mad if you hammer the old codger. So maybe the game should be played for lower stakes. Or maybe you should lose a little for Charlie's sake.

Should you beat your boss? Should you even invite your boss? Who gets into the game? When should you play? For what stakes? Think about these things, and we'll get back to them in the next few pages.

Your Opponents

Essentially, you choose your opponents, even when a game is hosted by someone else. The decision to sit or leave is always yours.

You'll learn a lot about poker if you play only with people who have superior skills. But you'll go broke paying for that education. Thus you should avoid sitting in a game when more than half the players are better than you. Ideally, the majority of your opponents should be loose and passive. Practically, you'll also see a fair number of over-the-top loose and aggressive players when the stakes are low. Of course, "low" is a relative term. Whatever the stakes, people tend to tighten up when they care about the money.

Give a table about thirty minutes, and if most of your opponents are playing well, then find a way to get out of the game. Or go into super-tight mode. Remember that winning pots and playing well are not necessarily synonymous. There is lucky, and there is good. Luck eventually turns. Good is forever.

Building a Game

Ask yourself the questions I posed at the beginning of the chapter, and then apply the answers to the following items.

The Lineup

Larger games are generally more exciting than smaller ones because there is more money in play and more personalities interacting. The more the merrier. Texas hold 'em and other flop games can comfortably handle up to ten or eleven players, though nine is a standard "full" table. Seven-card stud is best played with a maximum seven contestants (eight or more means you might have to reshuffle the discards in the middle of a hand). The energy at the table usually fades when the number of contestants drops to four or less. So it's best to have at least six or seven players in the game, so that people can take bathroom breaks, get beer, and so on without paralyzing the action.

If you're putting a game together, consider the factors I mentioned earlier. Choose people who have money, who are honest, who don't play too well, and who won't get on your nerves when the game goes into the wee hours.

Tip

If you host a poker game, be sure that everyone knows that you have veto power over who is invited. Your guests are not allowed to bring anyone in without your permission. In an established game that rotates among residences, the group usually votes as to who will be allowed in or invited back the next week.

Where, When, and For How Long?

You want a place that is inviting and convenient for the group. Some homes (and spouses) are more hospitable than others. So give this some thought. Pick a start time that is good for everyone, and be sure that every contestant knows that the group is counting on him to be there. It's frustrating to plan a poker game with seven people, and have three drop out at the last minute.

Most games last from three hours to…well…some games go for days, but three to six hours is standard. It's important that you set a time for the game to end, or you may have problems with some players wanting to continue indefinitely.

Necessary Equipment

It's best to have a big table and enough chairs to accommodate everyone. Of course, you don't absolutely "need" these things. I know a bunch of people who once played a killer game in a hotel suite on a standard bed. But generally, the contest is more fun when everyone is seated around a big table. If it has a cloth covering, even better.

At the absolute minimum, you need a deck of cards. However, it is customary to have two decks, each with a different colored back. This allows you to change decks if someone feels that a particular deck is "unlucky." The different colors prevent cards from one deck being accidentally mixed with cards from the other deck. Also, it helps to have a couple of new decks sitting around in case a card is bent or lost.

Show Us the Money

You can play with cash, but I don't recommend it. The stuff is awkward to handle unless all the bills are relatively new and flat. And do you want seven players toting $1,000 each to your house? Some people don't mind having thousands in cash floating around, but if you're not one of them, then poker chips are a better alternative.

Ideally, each player should have at least one hundred chips to start. Fifty to seventy-five of the chips should be of the lower denomination (whatever amount you choose), and the rest should be of the higher denominations.

Everyone buys in for a set amount, or you set up a system of accounting to record who buys in for what. Then you settle up at the end of the game, or at another pre-determined time (perhaps the beginning of the next game).

The general rule is that either cash or a check is acceptable for settlement, unless the winner specifically prefers one or the other. When possible, the debtor should try to pay in a form preferred by the winner.

Tip

It's okay to rake the pot to pay for food and refreshments, but you should resist the temptation to rake the pot for a profit. A regular rake for profit would put you in the position of being a gambling business, and most jurisdictions require such businesses to be licensed and regulated.

Drinks, Food, and Other Stuff

Pizza and beer, or caviar and champagne? You know what's best for your crew. Just make sure it's there for them. These goodies can be provided as a generous gift from the host, or everyone can contribute to foot the bill. Another option is to rake the pot for a dollar or two per pot until you reach the magic number.

Safety, Cheating, and Other Gritty Issues

Gambling games have a way of exposing our deepest emotions and desires. This is generally a good thing, being in touch with yourself. But some people may have problems with this intense experience. They have unresolved issues, dilemmas with money, self-esteem, control, or whatever. These issues may be dormant or unrecognized in casual encounters, but they can suddenly manifest themselves in the intense environment of the game.

Symptoms of problems can be anger, impatience, verbal abuse, violence, and of course, cheating. Hopefully, you've chosen opponents well, so none of these issues will come up.

But if something does happen, or you discover someone cheating, the best way to handle the problem is to diffuse it. Eject the offending player with as little fanfare as possible. End the game if you have to. Don't try to get even.

In some cases, it's better to let the game continue and simply exclude the player from future gatherings. Use your judgment.

A Few More Words About Cheating

Most people think of poker cheaters as card sharps who deal the best hands to themselves or their friends. This certainly happens, but it's not as common as other kinds of cheating.

Cheating usually takes the form of misdirection or collusion. Misdirection occurs when someone intentionally confuses the game to his advantage. An example would be someone who bets, and then when raised says, "I was just calling the bet ahead of me. What? He didn't bet, then I check, too."

THE FACT IS...

People who frequently use misdirection in poker games are known as "angle shooters." They think they're being clever, but in most cases they're simply being tolerated. Angle shooters tend to be long-term losers, because good players don't need to use tricky scams to make a profit.

Of course, the cheater's bet should stand. But sometimes the table lets him get away with it.

Another example of misdirection is someone who rushes the showdown to avoid a bet. Let's say it's down to three players. The first player checks. The second one is thinking when the third player suddenly flips up his cards and says, "I check, too. What do you have? What do you mean, you didn't check? I saw you check. Everyone saw you check."

If you're the second player, what are you going to do? Will you demand the pot without showing your cards?

Players who pull these little stunts are usually smart enough to mix them up, so it looks like general confusion rather than someone trying to save bets.

Collusion is a whole different scam. Two or more players use secret signals to communicate their hands to each other. This allows them to trap unsuspecting players in raising wars.

Let's say seat three is a poor sap with a king-high flush. Seat four has an ace-high nut flush. And seat one is in cahoots with seat four; he has nothing.

Seat one bets on the turn (with nothing). Seat three raises, seat four reraises, and seat one caps.

Then on the river, seat one bets. This time seat three calls (because he fears the nut flush). Seat four raises, seat one reraises, seat three calls, seat four caps it...and seat one folds! The two cheaters have screwed seat three out of multiple bets.

As with most scams, the scoundrels mix things up. They hit and then stop, so that fewer people will be suspicious. Signals can include coughing, tapping chips, scratching; there's no end to the creativity of cheaters.

As I mentioned previously, don't try to exact justice. Just cut your losses and exclude offenders quickly and quietly.

Oddball Rules

The official procedures for handling anomalies, such as accidentally exposed cards, are quite extensive. I won't cover them all, but here are the basics.

If two or more cards are accidentally exposed before "substantial action" (three players taking action) has occurred in a hand, then the hand is a misdeal. The cards are reshuffled and dealt again.

If only one card is exposed, the rules vary by game. In flop games, the card is shown to the table and used as the first burn card. In seven-card stud, the exposed card is used as the player's door card. In later rounds, cards that are exposed accidentally (usually while mucking) are shown to the table and sent to the muck.

In the last round of seven-card stud, there is no action between two players if one of them has an exposed last card. If there are three or more players in the final round, the player with the exposed last card has the option of being all in. In other words, his risk is limited to what he has already invested, and this creates a side pot for the last round. The all-in player can win the main pot, but not the side pot. If the player with the exposed card chooses not to take the option of being all in, then he can bet and raise in the final round as usual.

Shorthanded Play

I mentioned this in a sidebar in the last chapter, but I'm repeating it here because it's an important concept in home games. Strategy changes dramatically as the number of players decreases. Many more hands become playable. This is true in all poker versions. In hold 'em, you should be playing about 50 to 60 percent of your hands when the number of opponents gets down to three or four.

Pots are smaller, so drawing hands have less value, but big cards can often win without improvement. Thus you should call or reraise just about anything, from a premium hand to a bargain and some marginal trash, if you're in the blind. If you're under the gun, then you should raise about half of your playable hands and call with the rest.

The goal here is to nuke your opponent's pot odds. Calling should be expensive for him, and he should fear raising you because you will reraise.

Of course, if your opponent understands this, then he'll play back at you. Shorthanded games can be very exciting when two opponents are experts, but they can also be very expensive. If you're not willing to mix it up and take some chances, then don't play shorthanded.

Essentially

♠ You should avoid sitting in a game when more than half the players are better than you. Ideally, the majority of your opponents should be loose/passive.

♥ If it's your game, be sure that everyone knows that you have veto power over who is invited to compete. In an established game, the group usually votes as to who will be allowed in or invited back.

♦ Larger games are generally more exciting than smaller ones because there is more money in play and more personalities interacting. Flop games can comfortably handle up to ten or eleven players. Seven-card stud is best played with a maximum of seven contestants.

♣ Recommended equipment for your game includes table and chairs, two decks of cards, and one hundred chips for each player.

"It was a 'bluff' you know. At such a time it is sound judgment to put on a bold face and play your hand for a hundred times what it is worth; forty-nine times out of fifty nobody dares to 'call,' and you rake in the chips."

—Mark Twain, from his book
A Connecticut Yankee in King Arthur's Court

♠ If you have a problem with a player, eject him with as little fanfare as possible. End the game if you have to. Don't try to get even. In some cases, it's better to let the game continue and simply exclude the player from future gatherings.

♥ More hands become playable in shorthanded games. In hold 'em, you should be playing about 50 to 60 percent of your hands when the number of opponents drops to three or four. And many of those hands should be raised or reraised. If you're not willing to mix it up and take some chances, then don't play shorthanded.

CHAPTER 11

Gambling Debts and Other Stuff

The debt of honour must be paid.' These are the terrible words that haunt the gamester as he wakes (if he has slept) on the morning after the night of horrors: these are the furies that take him in hand, and drag him to torture, laughing the while...What a sensation it must be to lose one's all!"

So wrote Andrew Steinmetz, author of the 1870 gaming chronicle *The Gaming Table—Its Votaries and Victims*. Notice that he used the term "debt of honour." Did you know that gambling debts then (and now) are not legally collectable in most of the United States?

Let that sink in for a moment. Yes, I know this runs counter to everything you might imagine that you knew about gambling, so I'll explain how it works as we go along.

Also in this chapter, we'll talk about taxes on gambling profits and a few other things.

The Basics of Gambling Debt

Once upon a time in the medieval world, kings and the highborn had all the perks; everyone else was essentially chattel. Rights and privileges were assigned or allowed by those above. Period.

Thus there were few if any laws to "protect the citizens," or systems to assist individuals who might be in trouble. The remedies for catastrophe were charity, poverty, or slavery.

So let's say Charles got drunk one night and inadvertently gambled away his entire estate. Then he went double or nothing and lost his wife and children. Well, that would be that. The family would be broken up, Charles would be forever enslaved or indebted, and the winner (probably a highborn cheater) would be sipping brandy contentedly a few hours later.

A "Debt of Honour"

Of course, there were laws against gambling, but they rarely worked. People still gambled in defiance of the king and the Church. Besides, there was no legal system as we know it today to prevent upper-class winners from forcing lowborn losers to pay their debts (kneecap-busting goes back a long way). In situations when players were of equal social stature, the concept of a debt of honor insured that everyone settled up. To do anything less would cause the loser to be ostracized from society, and that exclusion would bring eventual poverty just as surely as handing over the farm.

Queen Anne and You

Then along came the merchant class and the beginnings of our modern money systems (checks, bank drafts, and so forth). Wise people in power began to realize that gambling with "ready money" is one thing, but gambling with debt is entirely something else. Clearly, transferring fortunes on a throw of the dice was not good for the economy. By the eighteenth century, laws were in force that made gambling debts uncollectable in most European countries. England's landmark legislation on this subject was the Statute of Anne (named after the English monarch on the throne at that time). Passed in 1710, it stated:

All notes, bills, bonds, judgments, mortgages, or other securities or conveyances...or other valuable thing whatsoever, won by gaming or playing at cards, dice, tables, tennis, bowls, or other game or games whatsoever, or by betting... shall be utterly void, frustrate, and of none effect, to all intents and purposes whatsoever....

Here's the important thing about the Statute of Anne. Almost anyone reading these words is still subject to this law three centuries later. That's because the U.S. system of jurisprudence is based on England's system, and nearly every state in the Union expressly incorporates English common law as a basis for local statutes. For example, Nevada's statute says:

> The common law of England, so far as it is not repugnant to or in conflict with the Constitution and laws of the United States, or the constitution and laws of this state, shall be the rule of decision in all the courts of this state.

Ditto for California, Michigan, etc... So gambling debts in the United States are not collectable unless a specific statute declares otherwise.

By the way, this isn't some crackpot taxes-aren't-legal hypothetical argument. In the last two centuries, there have been numerous state and federal court decisions that have upheld the Statute of Anne. A few of the big ones in recent years include *United States* v. *Wallace*, *Metropolitan Creditors* v. *Sadri* (in California), and *West Indies, Inc.* v. *First National Bank of Nevada* (in Nevada).

Simply put, Chuck can get drunk and gamble away his entire estate; he can sign whatever IOUs his opponents require, and then Chuck can walk away from his losses

without paying a penny. This is the common law unless a local law supersedes it.

You might think that the Statute of Anne would have brought the gaming industry to its knees centuries ago, but in fact, the reverse is true. The law had a beneficial effect because it encouraged responsible gaming. People who wanted to continue playing would pay their debts, and those who welshed were prohibited from playing, and thus excluded from further losing. Either way, welshers weren't prosecuted. Of course, loan sharks still cracked kneecaps, but that's the risk of dealing with criminals. In the legitimate gaming industry, or when playing with law-abiding citizens, the Statute of Anne has always been the rule, even in Nevada...until recently.

When Is a Loan Not a Loan?

In 1983 Nevada changed its statutes and made some gambling debts legally collectable. Casinos subsequently modified their markers and turned them into counter-checks. These days when you get a "loan" from a casino it's not really a loan. The marker you sign is actually a check. You have the option of later redeeming that marker with a personal check, chips, cash, or whatever. But the marker itself can be deposited against your checking account.

And if that marker bounces...well...Writing a bad check is a felony. These days, bad markers are turned over to the local district attorney. The D.A. then issues an arrest warrant that can be served anywhere.

So in some cases we're nearly right back to where we were in the beginning. Still, these days there is at least a nominal limit on the amount of debt that a casino player can accumulate.

Private Gambling Debts

How does all this affect you and your poker pals? The Statute of Anne is still the law in most places and in most circumstances. So you can't get drunk at a poker table and lose your house with an IOU. Your neighbor cannot sue you for the $5,000 that you lost playing poker last night. Well, actually, he *can* sue, but he probably won't win. Let's say that you bet your brother-in-law $10 million that it will rain tomorrow, but the day turns out to be sunny; your brother-in-law is not entitled to become an instant multimillionaire.

If someone writes a check and then stops payment, the issues may be somewhat more clouded (depending on the circumstances), but Vinnie from the body shop on the corner does not have the same legal standing as a licensed casino. Of course, fraud is against the law. That's a fact. And the legal system can be twisted ten zillion ways. But still, private gambling debts are generally not collectable.

 **Tip**

Don't write a check unless you're prepared to have that check deposited or cashed. It seems like a simple caveat, but people sometimes forget that checks are legal documents.

In 1776 (nearly seven decades after the Statute of Anne was enacted) an Englishman, Lord Carlisle, sent the following note to parliamentarian George Selwyn:

> I have undone myself, and it is to no purpose to conceal from you my abominable madness and folly, though perhaps the particulars may not be known to the rest of the world. I never lost so much in five times as I have done tonight, and am in debt to the house for the whole.

Lord Carlisle had incurred a "debt of honour," but in truth his honor would have been better protected had he played only with ready cash, and then stepped away from the table when his pockets were empty.

Gambling and Taxes

It's simple. You win money, you owe Uncle Sam. You lose money, that's your problem.

Gambling losses *can* be deducted, but only up to the amount of your gambling profits. So let's say you lost $10,000 this year. Well, that's just too bad. Better luck next time.

On the other hand, maybe you won $15,000 playing hold 'em and stud this year, but you got burned for $5,000 at the slots. You must declare the entire $15,000 you won. And if you want to deduct the slot loss, the IRS expects you to keep records, including the date and length of your sessions, the stakes, location, and similar info.

THE FACT IS...

Casinos report a player's gambling winnings to the IRS using form W2G (the player gets a copy of this form). But your gambling income is taxable even if it is not acquired in a casino or reported on a W2G.

But let's say you win $15,000 at 11 p.m. and lose $5,000 just two hours later, at 1 a.m. Do you have to declare the full $15,000 as income? Yes, if you received a W2G tax form for $15,000 from a casino, and then subsequently lost $5,000. But if the loss was during a poker session, you were up and then you were down in the course of two hours, then simply declare the net $10,000 profit. The IRS doesn't expect you to report every hourly bounce in a bankroll. But you must keep records.

As with all things involving taxes and government, there are a bazillion nuances to the law. Talk to a tax professional if you have questions about deductions or income.

The important thing to remember is that the IRS *will* ask questions about your sources of money if you are audited. So always declare your income.

Other Stuff

Poker is a big subject. Since this book is about playing poker at home, there is a lot of stuff about casino play that I didn't mention.

I'm going to list some of these items here; you can read more about them in *The Smarter Bet™ Guide to Poker* (Sterling Publishing).

The casino's rake: These are fees charged by a casino for providing the table and dealer. You have to beat your opponents *and the rake* to earn a profit.

Toking dealers: Tips are called "tokes" in the casino industry. There's a whole custom and strategy to toking.

Tells: An opponent's physical tics and other behaviors can give you clues as to what he is holding.

Casino strategy: The strategy for a full-table casino game is generally tighter and more aggressive than the tactics for a home game.

Other books in the *Smarter Bet™* series answer questions such as…What kind of swings in luck can I expect in a typical session? What is the optimal strategy for video poker? How can I win more when playing blackjack? Is there a way to predict how a slot machine will pay?

♠ *The Smarter Bet™ Guide to Slots and Video Poker*
   (Sterling Publishing)

♥ *The Smarter Bet™ Guide to Blackjack*
   (Sterling Publishing)

♦ *The Smarter Bet™ Guide to Craps*
   (Sterling Publishing)

♣ *The Unofficial Guide to Casino Gambling*
   (John Wiley & Sons)

Also, check out SmarterBet.com. This is an Internet site dedicated to all of the *Smarter Bet*™ guides. Here you'll find essays on poker strategy and information about other gambling contests, and you can drop me an e-mail and ask me questions.

Enjoy the game!

Essentially

♠ Private gambling debts between individuals are not collectable in most circumstances. The basis for this is English common law dating back to the Statute of Anne in 1710.

♥ A marker made out to a casino is not a loan; it's a check. Writing a bad check is a felony.

♦ Gambling income is taxable. Gambling losses can be deducted, but only up to the amount of your gambling profits. If you take deductions, then you must keep records.

♣ Check out the *Smarter Bet*™ guides and SmarterBet.com for more info about poker and other gambling games.

Glossary

action (1) Dollars wagered. More dollars is synonymous with more action. (2) A player's turn to act.

advantage player A player who uses strategy to gain an edge in a game.

all in Betting all of one's chips.

aggressive The characteristic of being more likely to bet or raise rather than check or call.

ante A mandatory first bet in seven-card stud and five-card draw.

backdoor flush In a flop game, a flush made with two suited cards on the turn and river.

bad beat An improbable loss.

bankroll An amount of money set aside specifically for wagering.

bicycle *See* wheel.

big blind *See* blind bet.

big cards Face cards and aces.

blank A card that has no effect on a hand; it does not help or hurt.

blind bet A mandatory bet in flop games. Typically, the two players to the left of the designated dealer post blind bets.

bluff To bet aggressively with a weak poker hand in an attempt to mislead opponents and cause them to fold.

board The poker table.

bring-in A mandatory first-round opening bet in seven-card stud. The bring-in is made by the player with the lowest exposed card.

burn To remove a card from the top of the deck without putting it into play. Burning one or more cards is a procedure to discourage cheating.

button Also known as a puck or a buck. A button is a marker that identifies the designated dealer in flop games. The button moves one player to the left after each hand.

buy in To exchange money for chips; to put money at risk in a game.

calling station A player who calls too much, a passive player.

call A bet that is equal to the previous player's bet.

cap A limit to the number of raises in a round. The limit is usually three or four raises.

cards speak A poker rule that requires winners to be determined by the cards and not by verbal declarations.

chase To call with a second-best hand.

check To offer no bet in a round that does not have a mandatory bet. A player who checks must call, raise, or fold if another player bets.

check-raise To check and later raise an opponent's wager in the same round.

closed poker Poker versions in which no cards are revealed before the showdown (as in five-card draw).

community cards Cards that are dealt face up and shared by all the players in a hand.

connectors Two cards of adjacent rank.

counting down The process of counting the money in a pot to determine that everyone has contributed the proper amount.

dead cards *See* live cards.

dealer (1) The person who distributes the cards in a poker game. (2) The position that determines action in a flop game (*see also* button).

defending the blind *See* steal the blinds.

designated dealer A rotating designation used to determine blind bets and the order of betting in Texas hold 'em and other flop games.

door card The first exposed card in a seven-card stud hand.

draw To surrender one or more cards and receive replacements from the dealer.

drawing dead Playing a hand that cannot win.

drawing hand A hand that is hoping to improve.

fixed-limit A poker game that allows bets only in specific increments of value.

flop (1) The three cards that are dealt face up on the table just prior to the second round of betting in a flop game. (2) The second round of betting in Texas hold 'em and other flop games.

flop games Poker versions with five community cards and four rounds of betting.

fold To surrender a hand and give up any claim to the pot.

foul To cause a poker hand to be invalid.

free card A card that comes "free" because there was no betting in the previous round.

gutshot straight draw A draw to an inside straight (needing exactly one rank rather than one of two).

heads-up Two players who compete after everyone else has folded.

hole cards The first two cards that àre dealt face down in Texas hold 'em or seven-card stud.

house edge The financial advantage a casino has in a wager.

implied odds The amount of a proposed bet compared to the expected future value of a pot. This is expressed as a ratio.

kicker The highest unpaired card in a poker hand when that hand is not a straight or flush.

limp in To call rather than raise the big blind in a flop game.

live cards Any cards that have not yet been exposed in seven-card stud.

live one A weak player; somebody who uses strategy incorrectly or not at all.

loose The characteristic of being likely to bet or call rather than fold.

muck To throw away cards. Also, the area where cards are discarded.

no-limit A poker game in which there are no restrictions on the amount that can be bet.

nuts Cards that make an unbeatable hand.

nut-flush A flush that cannot be beaten.

on-tilt A bad mood that adversely affects judgment and causes a person to play badly or erratically.

one player to a hand A poker rule that requires each player to make decisions alone and without consultation.

open poker Poker versions that use exposed cards (such as seven-card stud).

outs Cards that will improve a hand.

overcard In flop games, a personal card that has a higher rank than the cards on the board.

passive The characteristic of being more likely to check or call rather than bet or raise.

pocket cards *See* hole cards.

pocket rockets Two aces in the pocket.

post To place a bet (typically refers to a blind bet).

pot The combined bets of all the players.

pot odds The amount of a proposed bet compared to the amount in a pot. This is expressed as a ratio.

pot-limit A poker game in which any amount can be bet up to the amount in the pot.

protect your hand To handle cards in a way that reduces the possibility of the hand being fouled.

put an opponent on a hand An accurate guess of what an opponent is holding.

quad Four-of-a-kind.

rainbow Three or four cards that are not of the same suit.

raise A bet that is more than the previous player's bet. A raise requires all the other players in the hand to either call, reraise, or fold.

rake Money collected from players by a casino (or the host of a game). The funds are taken as a percentage of the pot, or as a flat fee.

river The final card and final round of betting in Texas hold 'em, Omaha, and seven-card stud.

rock An extremely conservative player.

scoop the pot To win both high and low in a high/low game.

semi-bluff Betting or raising with a weak hand when there is a good possibility that it can improve.

set Three-of-a-kind made with a pocket pair.

seventh street The final card and final round of betting in seven-card stud.

shorthanded A flop or stud game with five or fewer opponents.

show one, show all A poker rule that allows everyone at the table to see a player's hand if one opponent sees that hand.

showdown The end of the last round of betting in a poker hand when all remaining players reveal their cards.

side pot An extra pot that is created from bets made after a player goes all in to the main pot.

slow-play To play a strong hand passively, representing it as weak in order to keep players in the pot.

slow roll The slow reveal of a winning hand. This is a psychological tactic that is generally considered rude.

small blind *See* blind bets.

splashing the pot Throwing chips into the center of the table rather than putting them in front of one's position.

spread-limit A poker game in which there is a fixed minimum and maximum bet, but a player can wager any amount between those two figures.

steal the blinds To raise before the flop with a substandard hand in an attempt to get everyone, including the blinds, to fold.

street A betting round in seven-card stud.

string bet or string raise To call a bet, and then change it into a raise when an opponent appears to be weak. This is not allowed in most poker games.

steaming To bet in an aggressive way that disregards strategy. To be on-tilt and overly aggressive.

suited cards Two or more cards of the same suit.

table stakes A poker rule that requires all players to wager with only the chips that are on the table at the beginning of the hand.

tells Unconscious movements or body positions that indicate what a player is holding.

third street The first round of betting in seven-card stud.

tight A player who is averse to taking risks.

time A verbal request for a pause in the game.

toke Casino-industry jargon for a tip (gratuity).

trips Three-of-a-kind.

turn The third round of betting (fourth community card) in flop games.

under the gun The first player to act in a flop game.

weak The characteristic of being tight and passive.

wheel A low straight, ace through five.

wild card A card that can be used as a substitute for another card; a card that can be valued at any rank or suit.

Index

G

Games
    action ratio, 70–71
    betting limits in, 24–25
    big, 59
    blind bets, 25
    buy-in, 25
    fixed-limit, 24, 29
    no-limit, 25, 29
    organizing, 117–121
    position in, 53–54
    pot-limit, 29
    rounds, 29
    shorthanded, 58–59,
        122–123
    spread-limit, 24–25, 29
    standard, 59, 69
The Gaming Table—Its
        Votaries and Victims
        (Steinmetz), 125

H

Hands
    anatomy of, 26–29
    average, 50, 51, 54, 73,
        74, 75
    bad beat, 21
    bargain, 50, 51, 54, 71,
        73, 74, 75, 76
    big cards, 48–49
    borderline trash, 51

busted, 33
comparisons between, 51
connectors in, 49
drawing, 62, 81, 82, 86
drawing dead, 81
flush, 14, 16, 21, 22, 25,
    28, 49, 61
folding, 57–59
fouling, 32, 43
four of a kind, 14, 16
frequency of, 16
full house, 14, 16, 21,
    22, 62
gutshot straight draw, 52
judging, 47–53
losing, 58, 81, 86
marginal trash, 76
mucking, 32, 33, 34, 43
nut flushes, 22
nut straights, 22
pairs, 16, 49–50
percent probability
    of, 16
position and, 54, 72–74
premium, 50, 51, 54, 66,
    71, 72, 74, 75, 80
probabilities for
    improving, 61
protecting, 32, 43
ranking, 14–17
relative strength of, 57
revealing, 34

River, the, 27–28, 29, 37, 90–91

Robinson, Edward G., 29

Roulette, 10, 60

Rounders (film), 12, 20

Rules

    acting out of turn, 38–39

    card handling, 23, 31–32

    oddball, 121–122

    pulling the pot, 40

    revealing cards, 39

    seven-card stud, 97–101

    sharing hands, 39

    slow roll, 40

    splashing the pot, 37–38

    string bets, 38

    table stakes, 40–41

    table tapping, 40

S

Scramble, 34–35

Selwyn, George, 129

Seven-card stud, 13, 17, 19, 29, 97–101

    ante in, 23

    door cards in, 97–98

    double betting in, 99

later streets in, 100–101

    live cards in, 98–99

    pot odds in, 100–101

    starting hands in, 99–100

    streets in, 98

    suit in, 98

Showdowns, 13, 34

    judging winners in, 15

Shuffling, 23, 34–36

    casino-quality, 43

    cutting, 36

    finish, 36

    overhand, 35, 43

    riffle, 35, 43

    scramble, 34–35, 43

Skill vs. luck, 9–11

Slots, 10

Slow roll, 40

Southern cross, 108

Statute of Anne (1710), 126–129

Steamrolling, 52–53

Steinmetz, Andrew, 125

Straights, 14, 16, 21, 22, 51, 62

    gutshot, 52, 61

    nut, 85–86

Strategies, 4

    betting, 84–86

    casinos, 131